# Guided Grief Imagery

## A Resource for Grief Ministry and Death Education

*Thomas A. Droege*

PAULIST PRESS
New York ◇ Mahwah

The hymns "Lord, Take My Hand and Lead Me" and "Even As We Live Each Day" are copyright © 1978 *Lutheran Book of Worship* and are reprinted by permission of Augsburg Publishing House.

Library of Congress Cataloging-in-Publication Data

Droege, Thomas A. (Thomas Arthur), 1931-
    Guided grief imagery.

    1. Church work with the terminally ill.    2. Church work
with the bereaved.    3. Death—Religious aspects—
Catholic Church—Study and teaching.    4. Pastoral
theology—Catholic Church.    5. Catholic Church—
Doctrines—Study and teaching.    I. Title.
BV4460.6.D76    1987        259'.6        87-15520
ISBN    0-8091-2918-3    (pbk.)

Published by Paulist Press
997 Macarthur Boulevard
Mahwah, N.J. 07430

Printed and bound in the United States of America

# Contents

## Part I
## The Treasures of Faith Imagery
## for Facing Death

## Part II
## Exercises in Guided Faith Imagery

*To Esther, for faithful support
and loving presence*

# Introduction

There are few things more unique to us as human beings than the capacity to use our imagination. It's what distinguishes us from both animals and computers. We can use our imagination to solve problems and create new opportunities, but we can also use it to escape from reality. In the first case it is realistic imagery that we employ. In the second case it is fantasy. The process is the same, though the outcome is different. We applaud creative people for their vivid imaginations and assume that the pragmatic person who patiently plods through each day is unimaginative. Actually, the patient plodder may have powerful images by which he lives, however predictable they may be.

People tend to make broad generalizations about the use of imagination, many of which break down rather quickly. We have already noted one such questionable generalization in the above paragraph, the idea that some people are imaginative and others are not. Another closely related generalization, equally questionable, is that the imagination functions in a fairly uniform manner in all spheres of a person's life. The truth is that we may have a vivid imagination in one sphere of our lives and almost none at all in another sphere. Most men in adolescence and early adulthood are not lacking in their capacity to generate sexual imagery, some of it realistic but much of it fantasy. The same men at the same time of life are not likely to use their imagination at all when it comes to the experience of dying, neither their own dying nor the dying of others.

The imagination is particularly powerful in areas of experience and thought which we normally consider to be taboo. Sexuality is one example, and death is another. The power of the imagination, greater in such areas because there is so little interplay between the imagination and either private or public reason, can be put in the service of both good and evil. Pornography is an example of a distorted and sinful use of the imagination in the portrayal of sexuality. The violence of death in the media and the excessive masking of death in the funeral industry are examples of a distorted use of the imagination in the portrayal of death. What is needed in both areas is not more censorship but more positive uses of the imagination. We need to put the imagination in the service of faith. How do we accomplish that?

We have long known that the image we have of ourselves is the key to much of our behavior. We act in a certain way because of the way we see ourselves. That self-image, positive or negative, serves as a filter for what experiences we will allow to be integrated into our lives. How is this self-image changed? Not by insight and conscious determination to be different. It must happen in the way we imagine ourselves as loved, daring, competent. This is the truth in Norman Vincent Peale's much maligned ''power of positive thinking,'' which really ought to be called the power of a positive imagination.

If we can change the image we have of ourselves in creative ways, then we can also change our images of death. Images of death which evoke fear, anxiety, guilt, loneliness, anger, etc., can be transformed through a faith-full of the imagination. The Gospel provides a context within which faith can transform the image of death into an image of birth, seeing death not as an end but as a way of passage to life's completion. The purpose of this book is to activate the imagination in the service of faith as we encounter the reality of death and dying in our lives.

There is an assumption in the above paragraph which needs to be noted and made clear. The assumption is that faith works most powerfully at the level of the imagination. This book will not provide the reader with a theology of death though it is filled with theological reflections. The construction of a theology of death is primarily an intellectual task which could conceivably be done by someone who has no faith for readers who have no faith. It need only meet certain objective criteria, e.g., faithfulness to Scripture, internal coherence, etc. This book, by contrast, provides resources for activating the imagination of faith in contemplating the death of self and others. It is a hands-on pastoral care resource for grief ministry and death education.

The book is divided into two main parts. After an introductory chapter on the meaning and use of guided imagery, the first part is an exploration of the images of faith which Christians have used throughout the centuries in their encounters with death. Chapter 2 is a study of biblical images of faith and hope which sustained the people of God in both the Old and the New Testaments in their encounters with death. The thesis of Chapter 3 is that images of faith change in relation to the dominant fears of death in any particular historical period. Chapter 4 examines images of faith in the liturgy of the church, especially those liturgies which have death as their central focus, e.g., the funeral liturgy and the Easter vigil.

The second part of the book contains exercises in guided imagery for use by Christians, both privately and in groups. The purpose of these exercises is to activate the imagination of faith in its deeper-than-intellectual way of incorporating the experiences of death and dying into the wholeness and fullness of life. Chapter 5 introduces the second part of the book by providing detailed explanations on how to use guided imagery. Chapter 6 contains a series of exercises in guided imagery based on the psalms. The exercises in Chapter 7 are based on selected passages in the New Testament. Chapters 8 and 9 contain exercises for anticipating one's own death and grieving the loss of others. Chapter 10 contains exercises for the anticipation of losses throughout life.

My purpose in writing this book is to encourage the use of guided imagery by Christians within the context of the community of faith. This is intended as a practical book for use by ordinary Christians who are desirous of deepening their faith, especially in relation to experiences which are likely to provide the greatest tests of faith, namely, the various ways we encounter death. Parish leaders, both lay and clergy, will be able to use the exercises provided in this book by following the practical suggestions provided in Chapter 5.

The two parts of the book can be used independently. The same can be said for individual chapters. For example, one could make use of any of the exercises in guided imagery without reference to the first part of the book or to any other exercise. However, the guided imagery in the second part of the book is based on images of faith which were explored in the first part of the book. The use of those images will be much richer if one has given some thought to how they have been used in Scripture and the liturgy in different periods of history. On the other hand, material in the first part of the book could be used in an adult study group without making use of the exercises in guided imagery. However, the understanding of those images and the personal appropriation of them will be enhanced through the use of guided imagery.

I wish to express my appreciation to Dr. Robert Perry, Director of

Aquinas Center of Theology at Emory University, for introducing me to
the use of imagery through an experimental program of group spiritual
direction which he conducted in 1982. It was that experience which
prompted me to experiment with the use of guided imagery in classes I
teach at Valparaiso University on "Understanding Death and Dying." I
am grateful to my students for serving as experimental subjects for many
of the exercises which appear in this book. I am also indebted to Don
Tubesing, widely known as an author and trainer in the wellness movement, who provided both strong encouragement and practical guidance
at a crucial juncture in the completion of this project. He gave me many
useful suggestions for providing directions in the use of the exercises in
guided imagery. Finally, I express my gratitude to Elaine J. Ramshaw,
who was most helpful to me in providing data on hymn verses that relate
to death and dying.

Neither the research nor the writing of this volume would have been
possible had I not been the recipient of the O. P. Kretzmann Memorial
Scholarship which is awarded annually to a member of the V.U. faculty
for study in the healing arts and funded by the The Wheatridge Foundation. This foundation has a long and distinguished history of support
for healing within the context of the Christian faith.

Finally, I am deeply grateful to my wife Esther, to whom I dedicate
this book, for her faithful support of not only this venture but all of the
professional activities which have all too often absorbed time and energy
which rightfully belonged to her and our three children.

# 1. Guided Imagery: A Faith-Full Use of the Imagination

One of the primary assumptions of this book is that faith creates the images by which it lives. Faith begins with an experience of being in relation to God, such as being protected or guided in some special way. Images of faith give concrete and vivid expression to the experience. For example, the image of a shepherd gives expression to the experience of being protected or guided. Concepts like "guardian" or "guide" are higher level abstractions of what is embodied in the image of shepherd. At the highest level of abstraction the conceptual meanings are organized into the doctrine of the providence of God. This schema gives a certain priority to images in the "knowing" aspect of faith. It is the images which are closest to the experience and express it most vividly.

Images have always played a key role in the expression of faith. In the first half of the book we will examine the images of faith which have sustained Christians throughout history in their encounter with death. Scripture, liturgy, and pastoral care are the sources to which we will turn for images of faith. Those images have shifted somewhat over time in relation to the shifting imagery of death. What makes death frightening changes from one historical period to the next, and the images of faith which bring comfort and confidence change accordingly. It's not that the substance of faith changes, because faith is always rooted in the revelatory experience of God acting in Christ to save us from the power of death. However, the shape and the character of the images do change over time as faith searches for meaning in each new situation of personal and communal history.

If faith creates the images by which it lives, and if images are products of the imagination, then it should be possible to guide the imagination in its creation of images which give expression to our faith. Guided imagery is the term which describes this process. The exercises in guided imagery which comprise the second half of this book are designed to facilitate the construction of images of faith which grow out of the experience of our encounter with death and dying. A Christian does not construct images in the way God created the world—out of nothing. We have inherited a rich tradition of powerful images from which we can draw in exercises of guided imagery on death and dying. The purpose of the first half of this book is to name many, if not most of them. The challenge of the structured exercises of guided imagery is to relate the rich resources of imagery from the past to our own experience.

## A Faithful Use of the Imagination

How does the imagination work? Contemporary research indicates that human creativity is related to right-brain function, which includes spatial representation, metaphorical and pure melodic thought, visual and auditory imagery. By contrast, the left brain functions in linear, analytic, and rational modes. The scientific era in which we live has favored the analytical and rational modes of thought and denigrated right-brain activity as soft, ambiguous, and often misleading. That attitude is changing, however. Religious educators and therapists have been among the first to recognize the importance of enlisting the imagination to gain deeper entry into the inner world of human experience and thought.

The imagination is a natural resource that we all have for a fuller, more effective life. Rather than escaping reality, the imagination has access to the inner world of our experience and can give a deeper-than-intellectual expression to that reality. The capacity for creative daydreaming may be our most human quality, God's greatest gift. It allows us to relive the past and probe the future from the vantage point of our inner world in marvelously creative ways. We can experience a sense of inner peace, find comfort, or "scare ourselves to death" with nothing more than the material stored within the inner part of our being. For example, have you ever in times of stress imagined yourself to be safely cradled in the arms of a loving God? Such imagery can bring a soothing effect to every level of your being: physical, mental, and spiritual.

The most productive kind of thinking is always playing with possibilities through creative daydreaming. Reflect for a moment on the way you go about solving problems. You let your mind play with all kinds of possibilities until all of a sudden you say, "What if . . . ?" That's why the imagination is crucial for science as well as art. Every hypothesis is a product of the imagination. With art the process is even more obvious. The mind of an artist, like Picasso or Dostoevsky, is teeming with images searching for expression.

Not all imaginings are healthy, of course. A person can be so misled by her image of herself as being overweight that she becomes anorexic. It is realistic imagination rooted in experience that we must encourage, especially in matters of faith. A vision of life in heaven is an example of realistic imagination, not realistic like the painting of a landscape artist, but realistic in that it is rooted in faith and expresses an anticipation of continuity in one's life with God.

Keeping the imagination realistic is different from attempting to make the metaphorical literal. We need to learn to live with the image but be aware that we are doing so, resisting the rationalist tendency to translate what it can of the image into its categories and ignore the deeper reality that remains hidden to its more limited vision.

A realistic imagination is able not only to compose a past or future reality that has not been directly experienced (e.g., baptism or heaven), but it can recompose the world according to its terms. A good example is Jesus with the disciples on the road to Emmaus after his death and resurrection. With saddened hearts they looked back on the story of Jesus as a time of hope that had suddenly vanished. But their whole world is recomposed and suffused with life as they recognize Jesus in the breaking of the bread. In a similar manner, says William Lynch, we should "let Christ give us an image of the present."[1]

## The Use of Guided Imagery

Guided imagery is a method for letting Christ give us an image of the present. Mary Watkins provides a general description of what is involved in that process:

> The imagination is treated as if it were an internal place. One closes the eyes to the outside and gradually one begins to enter a sleeplike state of relaxation, as if one is travelling or falling into this interior space. Images begin to appear. At first they are fleeting and fuzzy as if one is on the outskirts of a town at dawn. Then clearer, more continuous. One believes that one sees the imaginal landscapes and figures as they really are.[2]

The process of guided imagery assumes the presence of a guide who forms an alliance with a person or group of persons to facilitate their experience of imagery. The guidance may be quite directive, suggesting concrete images for the person to reflect on, such as climbing a mountain or walking on a sandy shore. Or the guidance may be very indirect, leading persons to a deeper level of experience where they are encouraged to be open to whatever images spontaneously emerge.

The religious use of guided imagery heightens spiritual awareness, something for which people are hungering in an age dominated by science and technology. Religious rituals also activate the inner life of the spirit, as do events which prompt us to reflect deeply on the meaning of life. But there are few spiritual guides to help the average layperson to intentionally enter the inner life of the spirit to self-consciously reflect on the images which are born and nourished there. Most people do not know how wise they are, nor the depth and breadth of their visionary capacities, nor the rich imagery which is available to them from Scripture and tradition for finding meaning in their experiences of death and dying.

The hunger for spiritual awareness can be met by other than religious resources, of course, but religious resources are particularly significant for making meaning out of experiences of death and dying. The images of faith which have provided meaning for every generation of Christians will be described in earlier portions of this book. Those images might be called the depth dimension of religious beliefs, the importance of which is indicated in these comments of Ira Progoff:

> The nature of religious beliefs is such that, on the surface level, they can be stated by the rational mind and interpreted by means of intellect. But an inner experience of direct, nonrational knowing is essential in order to open the capacities of awareness at the deeper levels of reality to which the beliefs ultimately refer.[3]

There are ancient and respected traditions in Christianity as well as in other religions that have provided structures for meditating on the meaning of faith at levels deeper than the rational. Spiritual guides have been available since the dawn of Christianity to aid the devout in their spiritual journeys. In a culture which is so left-brain oriented and suspicious of all forms of interiority, a guide is needed to facilitate the exploration of inner space. Guided imagery is a medium for achieving that end.

We know that persons are deeply affected by their experiences of imagery. A person who in his "mind's eye" falls into a crevasse while climbing a mountain will experience physiological changes in temperature, brain waves, respiration, and heartbeat. Our bodies respond to what our imagination is focusing on. It is as if we were currently in the experience. A sense of panic may accompany the imagined struggle to free oneself from the mountain crevasse. The deeper the level of involvement in the imagined scene, the more vivid and enduring will be the images which accompany that experience.

Though everyone has a capacity for guided imagery, not everyone is an equally good candidate. Some people are not able to form visual images in their mind. Others are so solidly entrenched in the realm of the rational that they are either unaware or resistant to a journey into the realm of the imaginal. Still others fear the loss of control that is called for in allowing images to surface and submitting themselves to direction from an external guide. Even those who move easily into the realm of the imaginal will vary from time to time in their capacity for imagery, depending upon factors like stress, physical health, level of alertness, and time of day.

There is no way you can know in advance how good a candidate for guided imagery you might be. Understanding the process conceptually is not the same as understanding the inner dynamic of its operation. It is for that reason that the conceptual framework which I am providing in this chapter will be followed by exercises in guided imagery. I urge the reader not to make premature judgments about the use of guided imagery for oneself or others. Try it first.

## Guided Imagery as a Resource
## for Understanding Death and Dying

Most people have an uneasy feeling when they think about death, and they escape this feeling by submerging themselves in pressing issues of everyday life. But sooner or later, the question of the meaning of death forces itself to the forefront of attention. For some the reality of death comes crashing through the conventional cultural defenses in dramatic fashion. Someone close to you gets sick or dies. For others the question of death slowly seeps through to the level of consciousness with the realization that there are more yesterdays than tomorrows. Over half of life is already gone!

There is substantial evidence, however, that death denial is on the wane. The growth of the Hospice movement, TV documentaries, high school and college courses, and an abundance of literature on the topic herald a more open awareness of death and dying. How much better it is for people to intentionally raise the question of death rather than facing it as a life-trauma overladen with grief and/or feelings of high anxiety.

Guided imagery can be a helpful tool for heightening death awareness. I have discovered its value through teaching a course on death and dying to college students. There are several reasons why I have found it to be an effective learning tool. First, learning about death calls for more than intellectual mastery of subject matter. What one feels is as important as what one knows when a parent or close friend has died. Nor are catechetical answers sufficient when the issue is facing my own death. Dealing with death calls for whole person learning. There are a variety of exercises that one can use to facilitate deeper-than-intellectual learning, but I have found that guided imagery is a particularly helpful resource for this purpose.

Teaching students also helped me to discover that you cannot learn about death in general. Each person's way of approaching death is unique to that person, just as each person's style of living is unique. Guided imagery is a tool for exploring the inner world of experience without dictating in advance what one is to find there. A guide is useful for facilitating the entrance into that inner world and to suggest areas of exploration, but what one finds there will be unique to each person.

A third reason for the effectiveness of guided imagery is that it protects the privacy of the person, even when the exercises are done in a group setting. Because death must still be classified as a taboo subject in our society, most people are not likely to talk as freely about it as they would about their families, their jobs, their personal interests, or even their sexual activities. Guided imagery is a way of assisting people to explore the meaning of death without the expectation that they will share that experience with anyone else. Sharing of experiences can be enormously helpful, as anyone who has participated in a grief group will testify, but a deeply intrapersonal experience in a non-threatening group setting is the most useful tool that I have found to put people in touch with the felt sense of their fear and their faith in relation to death.

Finally, guided imagery is a good learning tool because it fosters the use of the imagination in an age when we have been taught from early childhood to value our rational powers more highly than our imagination. The faith of Christians is nurtured more by images than rational constructs. That's why story-telling is so effective in faith-building. The imagination can be guided to utilize the images of faith from Scripture and tradition to produce imagery that is effective in integrating the biblical story into the story of each person's own unique life.

## A Witness of Faith in an Age of Denial

The church has always played a prominent role in the care of the dying and the bereaved. Though modern day thanatologists, most of them psychotherapists, often speak of the art of dying as if they had discovered it and that they alone know how to lead people through it, it is the clergy who are the first to be called when a death has occurred or someone is dying. The Christian community has been and continues to be a primary support group for those who are facing death.

The church, more than any other institution in modern society, is in an ideal position to facilitate a deeper-than-intellectual understanding of the meaning of death. The death-denying tendencies of our modern culture have not reached as deeply into the life of the church as they have in other segments of our society. The fact that Christ's death is so central to the meaning of Christian faith ensures the presence of death imagery in the rites and practices of almost all Christian churches. Traditional Scripture readings, hymnody, and the liturgy are full of death imagery, especially in the season of Lent and Holy Week. It is to the church that people turn for comfort and hope in times of crisis. And so the church, more than any other institution of society, has the opportunity and responsibility to seek creative ways to engage people in an encounter with death that can produce a sense of hope and victory rather than a feeling of helplessness and hopelessness.

It would be a mistake, however, to underestimate the influence of the death denying tendencies in our culture, also on the church. It should not surprise us that death denial is strong among those whose identities are shaped by a secular society, and that includes all of us. There are very few resources in a secular society to quell the fear of death. To be secular is to define yourself within the limits of an empirical world, a world that can be seen, heard, touched, and measured. It is a wonderful world in which much can be accomplished. But it is a world in which everything must come to an end, and it is in the experience of the endings that we discover the roots of fear. Indeed, death casts a shadow over all of life in its reminder of the limits of a world that is defined exclusively in secular terms, and that shadow evokes fear. There is nothing to dispel that fear in a secular society because nothing within a secular world can overcome it. Death denial is precisely what we should expect in such a world.

The fear of death which lies at the very core of human selfhood goes far beyond simply a conscious feeling of fear at the thought of the future prospect of our biological death. The real fear is operating far below the level of conscious awareness and is so charged with terror that we simply cannot bear to allow it to come to full consciousness. The terror is always there below the surface, and it affects what we do, think, and feel in thousands of hidden and disguised ways.

The unconscious fear of death affects the life of the imagination as it does every other dimension of our personal lives. The repressive character of this fear does not mean that images of death no longer function within the sphere of our everyday experience. The problem is that they function independently, without the benefit of reflective reasoning in conscious awareness. The images of death are all the more powerful as a result.

How can we evoke those images without being overwhelmed by them? Only if we have images of faith which are more powerful. The center of the church's message is that death has been overcome. Why isn't that message more effective in countering the denial of death in our time? There are a variety of answers to that, but at least part of the problem is the ghetto mentality of the church. No matter how deeply one may understand the meaning of death in the biblical literature, it is not likely to make much difference unless that understanding addresses the problem of death denial at its core.

The church's imagery of faith and hope must be more powerful than the imagery of fear which is at the core of death denial in our culture. I am convinced that the battle will be won or lost at the level of competing imageries, where thought and feeling together shape attitude and practice. The exercises of guided imagery in this book are designed to engage people at the deepest level of their experience of both fear and faith with confidence that faith overcomes fear, even the fear of death.

## Overcoming the Fear of Death through Grief Ministry and Death Education

The record of the Christian church is quite good in its ministry to the grief sufferer during periods of crisis. The priest or pastor is likely to consider ministry to the dying as being high on the list of his or her priorities. When cure is no longer possible and care is at the heart of the prescribed treatment, clergy visits are eagerly anticipated in hospitals and hospices. When a death has occurred, the clergy are likely to be the primary care-givers. Not only do they preside over the funeral rituals, but they often orchestrate the response of the community of faith to the loss of one of its members.

The exercises in guided imagery in this volume are intended as an additional resource to enhance the grief ministry of church leaders. Grief ministry is needed not only by those who are experiencing a significant loss, but also by those who are anticipating such a loss. That includes everybody, of course, when anticipatory grief is conceived of in its broadest sense. Such broad definition of anticipatory grief comes closer, however, to what I mean by death education. A grief ministry for those anticipating a loss is directed to the close relatives and friends of persons with a terminal illness. A number of exercises in Chapters 8 and 9 are specifically designed for grief ministry, but many others could easily be adapted for that purpose.

The record of the church has not been as good in preparing people for facing the deaths that all of us must face at some point in our lives. Too often has the church mirrored the cultural denial of death and dying. The church ought to be in the forefront of death education, and in some ways it always has been. References to death and dying are plentiful in Scripture, hymnody, and the liturgy. However, most of the time those references are in the background as general truths and get focused as personal issues only when a death occurs. Death education has not been a prominent part of the curriculum of either parochial or Sunday schools.

For all of these reasons, a vital ministry in death education is badly needed in our secular, death-denying society.

The purpose of a program in death education is to help the participants of that program integrate the meaning of death and dying into their lives. People need help in identifying resources within themselves and their faith tradition to cope with the inevitable losses that are part of any life, and especially the major losses experienced in the death of loved ones and in the anticipation of one's own death. There are many different kinds of exercises that can be used to facilitate a deeper-than-intellectual awareness of death and dying, guided imagery being only one. However, guided imagery is particularly effective for that purpose.

The context of a program in death education assumes, for the most part, that those participating are not at the time experiencing a serious loss. The goal is preventive rather than curative. Death education is a wellness program in that learning to cope with experiences of death and dying is part of a healthy life-style. Indeed, a wellness workshop that does not include at least one exercise in death awareness is not complete. Those who are undergoing the trauma of a recent loss or are anticipating a loss in the near future have different needs. A person who is terminally ill and another who is twenty-five and in the best of health can both benefit from an exercise in imaging their death, but two different exercises are called for. So also for those who are grieving the loss of a loved one. There is a qualitative difference between a loss experienced last week and one experienced twenty years ago, and an exercise in guided imagery should reflect that difference.

Hopefully, books like this one will prompt churches to recover their heritage and reassert their rightful leadership in the field of grief ministry and death education. A church building with its powerful symbols of cross and resurrection provides a much better environment for learning about death and dying than a high school or college classroom. The church has ready access to images of faith and hope which have sustained Christians in their grieving and dying throughout the church's history.

One of the purposes of this book is to reclaim the imagination as a gift of God and a resource for faith. We can use our imagination to move freely from the present to either the past or the future. When used as a resource of faith, the imagination can help us to anticipate both the experience of dying and the fullness of life which awaits us beyond death. Both Scripture and the liturgy are full of images of faith which are the product of the imagination of faith in response to the revelation of God. We will use those images and cultivate images which grow from the seedbed of our own experience in the exercises of guided imagery which form the second portion of this book.

## Notes

1. William F. Lynch, *Images of Faith* (Notre Dame: University of Notre Dame Press, 1973), pp. 140f.

2. Mary Watkins, *Waking Dreams* (Dallas: Spring Publications, 1976), p. 143.

3. Ira Progoff, *At a Journal Workshop* (New York: Dialogue House Library, 1975), pp. 48f.

# *Part I*

# The Treasures of Faith Imagery for Facing Death

# 2. Biblical Imagery for Facing Death

In this chapter we will examine the rich resources of biblical imagery that can be used in grief ministry and death education. The purpose of this chapter will not be to provide the reader with an overview of biblical ways of understanding death. That has been done by others in more or less systematic ways, either by examining a particular book of the Bible or by tracing themes which emerge in the Old or the New Testaments.

A ministry to those who are facing death, whether in a crisis situation or not, must engage people at the level of their experience. It's not a theology of death which they need so much as stories of faith and images which express that faith. And so we turn to the Bible with a particular set of questions about the fear of death which is expressed by the biblical authors and the faith with which they countered such fear. What are the images of death in the stories which reflect the experience of the people of God? What is frightening about these images? What is the content and the structure of faith that brings hope and comfort in the face of this fear? What are the images which express that faith?

Carefully conceived concepts are necessary building blocks for the construction of a theology of death, but images are closer to the level of experience and can more faithfully capture the felt sense of that experience through an imaginative use of the mind. That's why imagery is so important for this book. In the next three chapters we will be concentrating on the imagery which we inherit from Scripture and the church's tradition. In the guided imagery exercises that make up the second half of the book we will be using the imagery which is part of our inheritance of faith as well as constructing new imagery which reflects the experience of our own age, some of which we share in common and some of which is unique to our own life stories.

## Genesis 3

"You are dust, and to dust you shall return." The story of Adam and Eve in the Garden of Eden makes it clear that the awareness of death has been part of the consciousness of humanity from the very beginning of recorded experience. However, there is no evidence in the account that death belongs in the order of creation as God originally planned it. It is referred to only as a contingency within that plan, a contingency which would be invoked if Adam and Eve fail to be the kind of people which God intends them to be. So says Eve to the serpent: "We may eat of the fruit of the trees of the garden; but God said, 'You shall not eat of the fruit of the tree which is in the midst of the garden, neither shall you touch it, lest you die' " (Gen 3:2–3). Death will be a part of their (our) experience only if and when sin becomes the worm at the core of human existence.

That does not mean that death comes as a punishment for sin. Quite the contrary. Death is God's no to a never-ending life which is worm-infested at the core. God sends Adam and Eve from the Garden of Eden and bars their way back so that they will not eat of the tree of life and live forever. To live forever is no blessing in a sin-cursed world. Death provides a merciful limit to that kind of distorted existence.

Adam and Eve do eat of the forbidden fruit, as each of us has done in our own way. God speaks to them about what human experience will be like under the conditions of sin. Neither the womb nor the land will yield its fruit with ease. "In the sweat of your face you shall eat bread till you return to the ground, for out of it you were taken; you are dust, and to dust you shall return" (Gen 3:19). A shadow has fallen across the world, a shadow which reaches over all of life, including its ending. What would dying have been like in the Garden and thus within the goodness of God's creation? That we cannot answer because there is no memory from the past or anticipation of any future in this life which could provide an answer. We know only about an experience of dying which is touched by the curse of sin.

What imagery of death emerges from this time-honored story? There is imagery of dying away from home and separated from the person you need the most. Adam and Eve belong in the garden which God had created for them, but they die east of Eden, away from home and separated from the God who is the source of their life and hope. The fear of dying away from home, home being where God is, can be found throughout Scripture. It was the fear of the Israelites in the period of the exile, cut off from the land of promise by the judgment of God. It was the fear of the psalmist who images death as Sheol, the one and only place where God could not be praised. It was the fear of Jesus, for whom death was an experience of being forsaken by God. And it is the fear of the Christian when anticipating standing before the judgment seat of God.

There is also imagery of disintegration and decay in this story. "You are dust, and to dust you shall return" (Gen 3:19). God formed Adam "of dust from the ground, and breathed into his nostrils the breath of life" (Gen 2:7). Death comes when the breath (the spirit) of God has left Adam, at which time the body which began as dust becomes dust again. There is no hope of reincarnation here, no participation in the eternal cycle of nature. Instead the imagery of "dust to dust" links humanity to every other living thing within the order of creation. We are born. We live and flourish. We wither and die. In our biological beginnings and endings we are no different than a blade of grass or a grasshopper. We spoke in Chapter 1 of the fear of death which permeates our secular society. Would there be such fear if sin had not entered the picture? We have no way of knowing from this story because the imagery of death and sin's consequences are so closely linked. However, St. Paul tells us that the sting of death is sin, prompting Luther to say that death without sin would have no more terror than a snake without its poisonous viper.

### Genesis 22

"Abraham . . . took the knife to slay his son." The story of Abraham and Isaac is a story about death, though what makes it frightening is different for him than it is for us. What we fear about death is that it brings "little me" to an end. Our faith is in the hope of the resurrection, God's promise in Christ of safe passage to the other side. For Abraham it was different. What he feared in death was not the loss of self but the loss of his son because the promise that he trusted was the promise that his heirs would be as numerous as the stars in the heavens.

As long as that promise was sure, Abraham had no fear of death, as is obvious in the description of his death: "Abraham breathed his last and died in a good old age, an old man and full of years, and was gathered to his people'' (Gen 25:8). The only threat of death in the story of Abraham is the death of Isaac, the son of promise. Abraham could face this threat, which was much more terrifying than a threat to his own life, only by trusting in a promise of God which seemed to be negated by the command of the very same God to sacrifice his son.

The image of death in this story is that of a knife poised over an altar-bound Isaac. A knife at his own throat would have been a blessing by comparison. Abraham wasn't bothered about the future of ''little me'' as we are. He was to be the father of a great people. That's what gave his life meaning and purpose.

The point of this story is that Abraham's trust in the promise of God remains sure even when the terror of death attacks the very core of the promise. Luther's commentary on Genesis is helpful in understanding this point. He placed this thought in the mind of Abraham: ''I am reducing my son to ashes. Nevertheless, he is not dying. Indeed, those ashes will be the heir.''[1] How can Isaac be both dead and the heir who will have children through whom the whole world will be blessed? Because God has promised it and because faith holds on to that promise even in the face of evidence that totally contradicts it. So reasoned Luther.

Luther put the same statement of faith into the mouth of Isaac: ''God will not lie. I am the son of the promise. Therefore I must beget children, even if heaven collapses.''[2] Nothing less than the structure of the universe is at stake here. Take away the promise and everything collapses. Better yet, even if the structure of the universe collapses, the promise of God is still certain.

So it is, Luther went on to say, with our own death. How can one possibly believe that death is not death but life? All of the evidence would suggest that in the midst of life we are in death. The Gospel, however, inverts the statement to say that in the midst of death we are in life. So attests St. Paul in 2 Corinthians 6:9: ''As dying, and behold we live.'' On this Luther commented: ''This is the power of faith, which mediates in this way between death and life, and changes death into life and immortality, which, as faith knows, has been bestowed through Christ.''[3] It is only the death and resurrection of Christ that can ultimately reconcile the opposites of death and life which loom so large in the story of Abraham and Isaac.

As is obvious in the above interpretation of the story of Abraham and Isaac, there is a blending of images: the images of Abraham and Christ, the images of Mount Moriah and the Mount of Calvary, the images of father Abraham and father God. These are powerful images at the very center of a faith rooted in the promises of God. Their power is in their capacity to express the confidence that nothing can undo or invalidate the promise of God, not even God himself. And the promise of God is that the last word is not death but life.

## The Psalms

Death is imaged in many different ways in the psalms: abandonment, a snare, a shadow, sinking slowly into a pit, dwelling in the shadowy regions of Sheol, and being sucked into a watery chaos. Yahweh, who provides comfort and hope to those who experience the terror of dying, is imaged as: father, mother, nurse, friend, shepherd, physician, rock, fortress, shield, and stronghold. The exercises in the second half of this volume will draw heavily on the richness of the imagery in the psalms. What follows in this section is a descriptive commentary on that imagery.

Many of the psalms are written out of the experience of pain, disappointment, and feelings of abandonment. Those experiences were particularly painful when the psalmist perceived himself as approaching death because he believed that death brought the end of his relationship to God. Beyond death lay Sheol. Only with an audacity of faith rare even among the faithful of Israel would one think, much less hope, that Yahweh, the God of life, might enter this shadowy realm of lifelessness and nothingness. The cries of lament in the psalms are full of the fear of the absence of God as well as a hunger and a thirst for the presence of God. Far from a triumphal faith that knows neither despair nor need, the psalmist pleads for help in the midst of great uncertainty and deep fear. The intensity of the desperation, however, is matched by the intensity of hope in the promises of God. From such intensity of both hope and fear come images which can put us in touch with our own experience and our own creative capacity for image making.

### Valley of the Shadow—The Lord as Shepherd

The imagery is familiar to every Christian: "Even though I walk through the valley of the shadow of death, I fear no evil; for thou art with me; thy rod and thy staff, they comfort me'' (Ps 23:4). What is the story behind the image of "the valley of the shadow of death"? Might it not be a shepherd guiding his flock from one pasture to another through a narrow valley set between two tall hills? It is late in the afternoon, and suddenly a wolf appears at the top of one of the hills. The late afternoon sun casts a huge shadow of the wolf on the hill that stands on the other side of the valley. That is the "valley of the shadow of death." If the shepherd weren't there, fear would scatter the flock in every direction. They would be easy prey for the enemy. I have sometimes felt that a hospital corridor is like a valley over which the shadow of death falls. One senses the presence of the wolf, so much so that some find it hard to even enter a hospital. Yet the shepherd is there as well, and that brings comfort and reassurance.

### Watery Chaos—Safe Passage

Water is a symbol of chaos in Scripture from the very first chapter: "The Spirit of God moving over the face of the waters" is an image of God bringing order out of chaos. So also the psalmist speaks of "a time of distress, in the rush of great waters" (Ps 32:6). Close to death, the author of Psalm 69 cries out: "Save me, O God! For the waters have come up to my neck. . . . I have come into deep waters, and the flood sweeps over me. . . . Let not the flood sweep over me, or the deep swallow me up, or the pit close its mouth over me" (Ps 69:1–2, 14).

Yet faith has confidence that the God who brought order out of chaos at the beginning of time will continue to do so until the end of time:

> When the waters saw thee, O God, when the waters saw thee, they were afraid, yea, the deep trembled. The clouds poured out water; the skies gave forth thunder; thy arrows flashed on every side. The crash of thy thunder was in the whirlwind; thy lightnings lighted up the world; the earth trembled and shook. Thy way was through the sea, thy path through the great waters; yet thy footprints were unseen. Thou didst lead thy people like a flock by the hand of Moses and Aaron (Ps 77:16–19).

The memory, of course, is the exodus and the mighty deliverance of Yahweh through, not around, the watery chaos. This treasured memory of the community was also a source of private comfort. If Yahweh could lead the whole people of God through the watery chaos to the other side, surely he can be counted on for deliverance in periods of personal distress.

What brings comfort is an image of passage, going through a threatening time or place and coming out safely on the other side. The safe passage of Israel through the watery depths prefigures the paschal mystery of Christ's death and resurrection, God's ultimate act of deliverance from death. Paschal imagery is at the very center of the Christian understanding of death, especially in the sacrament of baptism, whose waters, like the waters of the Red Sea, are a passageway from death to life.

### Abandonment—Presence

Images of abandonment and presence are perhaps the most deeply rooted images of human experience, reaching all the way back to the terror that a small child feels at the thought that mother or father just might not come back—ever. The image of being abandoned by God at the time of death is closely linked to the primal terror of a small child being abandoned.

The psalms of lament are full of abandonment imagery. Two examples will suffice. "As with a deadly wound in my body, my adversaries taunt me, while they say to me continually, 'Where is your God?' " (Ps 42:9–10). Like any taunt, the question is bothersome because it is the psalmist's own question. "How long, O Lord? Wilt thou forget me for ever? How long wilt thou hide thy face from me? . . . Consider and answer me, O Lord my God; lighten my eyes, lest I sleep the sleep of death" (Ps 13:1–3). No one wants to go to sleep feeling abandoned, particularly if it is the sleep of death.

If the image of abandonment is rooted in the earliest of childhood memories, so also is the image of presence. In the experience of most children parents do come back after periods of absence, both short ones and long ones. Their presence can be counted on. Out of such experience is born the trust on which all the rest of human experience must build, including the experience of the presence of God. The faith of the psalmist in the presence of Yahweh reaches back to the earliest of experiences, even before the time of birth: "For thou didst form my inward parts, thou didst knit me together in my mother's womb. . . . Wonderful are thy works! Thou knowest me right well" (Ps 139:13–14). If the presence of

God was there from the beginning, even prior to birth, then it is not fool-
ish to believe that one will not be abandoned in the end—not even in
Sheol! With the audacity of faith the psalmist can say: "Wither shall I
go from thy Spirit? Or wither shall I flee from thy presence? If I ascend
to heaven, thou art there! If I make my bed in Sheol, thou art there" (Ps
139:7–8).

### Terror—Trust

Images of terror and trust abound in the psalms, and they almost
always appear in relation to each other. The images of terror take many
forms: an earthquake that makes the mountains shake, a storm that
causes the waters to roar and foam, a deadly disease that brings one to
the gates of Sheol, being caught unexpectedly in the snare of a fowler,
being pursued by an enemy whose goal is your destruction, walking
through a valley of the shadow of death, being abandoned in a dark and
deep pit, being hit by an arrow. Not all of these images are directly related to dying, but death is the ultimate threat which lurks behind each
of them. "My heart is in anguish within me, the terrors of death have
fallen upon me. Fear and trembling come upon me, and horror overwhelms me" (Ps 55:4–8).

The counterpart to terror, that which finally quells it, is trust. Our
relationship to God begins and ends with trust, and in times of terror it
is trust which is at the center of faith. Nowhere is that more obvious than
in the psalms. "The Lord is my light and my salvation; whom shall I
fear? The Lord is the stronghold of my life; of whom shall I be afraid?
. . . For he will hide me in his shelter in the day of trouble; he will con-
ceal me under the cover of his tent, he will set me high upon a rock" (Ps
27:1, 5). With terror come feelings of littleness and helplessness, but the
"shadow of the Almighty" evokes a feeling of trust. "For he will give
his angels charge of you to guard you in all your ways. On their hands
they will bear you up, lest you dash your foot against a stone" (Ps 91:11–
12).

### Ezekiel 37:1–14

"O dry bones, hear the word of the Lord." The imagery of the
psalms is easy to identify with because the experiences of the psalmist

are so much like our own. The imagery of death in Ezekiel is not so easy to identify with because the experience of communal annihilation of which he speaks can only be imagined. The threat of nuclear war is sufficient to awaken our need for imagery that would sustain us in the loss of our communal identity.

Ezekiel speaks out of the experience of the exile, when Israel was cut loose from all the anchors of their identity as a people of God: land, king, and temple. He finds himself in the middle of a valley of dry bones. The bones are the bones of the whole house of Israel, and Israel's hope is as dead as those bones. But death is not to have the last word. God causes flesh to come upon the bones and skin to cover the flesh, and God breathes his spirit into them as he did into Adam at the beginning of the world. The dry bones become living people, a great host of people.

The experience of Ezekiel in the valley of dry bones is the same as the experience of Abraham on Mount Moriah. In both cases it was the promise of God to the people of Israel that was threatened, in one case by the death of Isaac and in the other by the death of Israel as a nation. As was true in the Abraham narrative, Ezekiel's imagery calls for radical faith in the promise of God in spite of all the evidence which points to the demise of that promise.

What would become of our faith in a nuclear holocaust? Would we find imagery as powerful as that of Abraham and Ezekiel to sustain us? The questions are unpleasant, even unthinkable. But we would not be faithful to the biblical witness if we did not raise those questions and look deeply into ourselves for the imagery of faith which would sustain us.

## 1 Corinthians 1:23

"We preach Christ crucified." Of all the world religions only Christianity has an image of death as its central symbol. To rediscover the full imagery of death that the cross represents, we need to return to the Gospels, especially the Gospel of Mark. The fear of death which is evoked by the image of the cross is expressed by Mark with striking realism, and it is clear that Jesus experienced the fear as well as his followers. The fear was that Jesus' death meant defeat, the powerlessness of God, the victory of Satan, and the establishment of death's reign. If the valley of the dry bones is an image of the death of Israel in the exile, then the cross is an image of the death of the whole cosmos.

Rarely do we allow ourselves to experience the full power of death which is imaged in the cross. Rarely do we let ourselves contemplate how close to the teetering edge of chaos our world came in this event. Rarely do we see the image of the cross as an image of the death we deserve. Rarely do we see the cross as the moment of Death's greatest victory and Life's greatest loss.

The power of death must have seemed omnipotent to Jesus on Calvary unless we assume that his deity rendered death more impotent for him than it is for us. Jesus is called "the pioneer and perfector of our faith" (Heb 12:2) because on the cross he is a better example than even Abraham of faith which sustains in the throes of the deepest kind of existential anxiety, an anxiety which floods the heart and soul when the promise by which one lives seems to be under the threat of extinction. Though feeling abandoned, forsaken even by God, Jesus calls out "My God," trusting in the promise that he was indeed the "beloved Son" that his Father in heaven had called him at his baptism.

The cross which stands behind the altar in the Chapel of the Resurrection at Valparaiso University is called Christ the King. It depicts Christ on the cross, but with the crown of a king rather than a crown of thorns, and with arms outstretched in victory rather than being nailed to the cross in defeat. This is imagery of life bursting forth from death, victory from defeat, strength from weakness, and the power to save from suffering. Such imagery is a helpful reminder that God chose death as the means by which to end death's reign of terror, that the images of the cross and the empty tomb are inextricably intertwined, that there is no way around death, but only a way through it.

### Matthew 28:5–6

"He is not here; for he has risen." With the resurrection of Jesus the tomb becomes an image of a new beginning rather than an image of the end of life. There is no denial of death here, no suggestion that death is anything other than the end of life as we know it. And yet the tomb is empty and the promise filled full. The empty tomb becomes the image of every tomb that has a cross standing over it. There is no denial of death in a Christian burial, either of its realism or its finality. The empty tomb, first Christ's and then ours, images a new reality which reaches beyond the finality of death.

I'm not sure that we should ever try to get too far beyond the image of the empty tomb. All images of life after death are highly speculative and say more about the power of our imagination than they do about the reality which they are attempting to express. All of the Gospel that we need to know is imaged in the empty tomb. The power of death is broken and the promise of life with God is sure. What more do we need to know? Too often the striving for images which are realistic representations of what lies beyond death is prompted by a need for evidence that will count as proof of a hereafter. All we have for sure is the promise, and the promise is imaged in the empty tomb.

## Mark 8:35–36

"Whoever loses his life for my sake and the Gospel's will save it." One of the inevitable components of dying is surrender, the surrender of self and all that the self holds dear. There are two types of surrender. One is involuntary, surrendering that which is dear to us when losing it is beyond our control. The other type is voluntary, surrendering what is dear to us for the sake of another. Jesus is talking about the latter kind of surrender, but the two kinds are closely intertwined in relation to the dynamics of grieving.

The surrender called for in dying is giving up one of our primary needs, the need to be in control. Surrender means accepting the loss of physical control over bodily functions in the process of aging and dying. Surrender means letting go of all the possessions we worked so hard to secure: home, care, clothes. Surrender means letting go of the goals which have given meaning and purpose to our lives when premature death will not allow us to achieve them. Surrender means letting go of loved ones who have filled our lives with joy. Finally, surrender means letting go of a childish (not childlike) dependence on a God who will always do what we want.

The surrender called for in sacrifice is no different from the above, except that it is voluntary and thus infinitely harder. It is voluntary surrender that Jesus had in mind when he said that losing your life for the sake of the Gospel is saving it. Voluntary surrender may mean the sacrifice of life itself, as it was with Jesus. But most of the time it is the surrender of lesser things, such as possessions and power—sacrificial mini-deaths prompted by faith in him who gave his all that we might live.

Both types of surrender are acts of faith, calling for confidence that the God of the cross will not desert us. A lifestyle of voluntary surrender will lead naturally and easily to the involuntary surrender called for in dying. There will be exercises in guided imagery to facilitate such surrender.

## Romans 6:3–4

"We were buried . . . with him by baptism into death." St. Paul uses the core image of the Christian faith, death-resurrection, to express how we by baptism become embedded in Christ, embedded both in who he is and what he did. The mode of baptism which represents the image most faithfully is immersion. Going under the water is both a washing and a drowning. The first breath in coming out of the water is like the first breath of an infant who emerges from a watery womb. There is an advantage to matching the mode and the imagery of baptism, especially for adults, but the participatory imagery retains its meaning and power no matter what mode of baptism is used.

To be baptized is to die with Christ the only death that really counts. It is the death of sin, the death that has a sting to it, the death that creates terror because it makes for our estrangement from God. Jesus died the death of sin on the cross, and our baptism is a participation in his death and resurrection. To be baptized is to be cradled in the arms of the risen Christ and covered with the cloak of his righteousness. The baptismal pall which is placed over the casket at the funeral service of a Christian makes that image very concrete. Covered with the life of Christ, the Christian who has died shares in the paschal mystery of Christ's death and resurrection, a passage which can be celebrated by the community with songs of Easter joy. We will make extensive use of this imagery in the exercises to follow.

Eternal life is a life which begins with baptism, not with physical death. It begins there because in baptism eternal death has been dealt with finally and fully. To be baptized means that "I have been crucified with Christ; it is no longer I who live, but Christ who lives in me" (Gal 2:20). That doesn't mean that I am death-proof, but it does mean that my life is so deeply rooted in Christ and his promise that the primary threat of death, separation from God, has been eliminated.

## Matthew 25:31–46

"He will separate them one from another as a shepherd separates the sheep from the goats." In Christian consciousness the fear of death has always been associated with the fear of judgment. The fear of God's judgment has been greater in some periods of history than others. It reached its peak in the late medieval period and was very pronounced at the time of the Reformation. The fundamental question in Luther's theology, "How can I find a gracious God?" was prompted by the fear of judgment. That question has faded into the background for most contemporary Christians, but it is never entirely absent from the minds and hearts of Christians in any age.

Jesus himself provides us with the imagery of judgment which has molded Christian consciousness more than any other. He speaks of the Son of Man sitting on a royal throne with all the nations (not just Christians and Jews) gathered before him. The king (judge) divides the throng into two groups, one to share in the reign of Christ through all eternity and the other doomed to eternal punishment. The criterion of judgment is simple. Members of the one group fed the hungry, clothed the naked, and visited the sick, each of whom was Jesus in a form they could not recognize. Members of the other group had similar opportunities, but failed to respond with acts of charity.

Part of the power of the imagery is its simplicity. There is no ambiguity. You are either saved or damned. The power of the imagery is also in the personal character of the charity involved. Rather than ethical principles or rules of conduct so dominant in the complex ethical analysis of social issues, there are only stories about how one person treats another. That imagery is made all the more striking in that Jesus identifies himself with the plight of the hungry, the naked, and the sick. These are not nameless, faceless victims on whom acts of charity are bestowed. Each has the name and face of Jesus.

One can focus on either the positive or the negative in this imagery. In the darkest days of the Middle Ages, the focus was almost exclusively on the side of images of frightening punishment in the forms of fire, torture, and endless suffering. We will look at some of those images in closer detail in the next chapter. The intent of the imagery, however, would seem to be in the opposite direction. Our lives are filled with opportunities to express our faith (Christ in us) through our actions, particularly in relation to other persons in need of our care. Jesus is on both sides of that action, both in the receiving and in the giving. We are urged by this imagery to seize the opportunities that we have, for the time is short and there will be no second chance.

### Revelation 21:1–4

"He will wipe away every tear from their eyes, and death shall be no more." The Gospel of John and the Revelation of John both use the imagery of "dwelling with God" to picture what lies beyond the gates of death, but they do so in different ways. In John 14:2–6 Jesus invites us to share the dwelling place of his Father in heaven, a home with many rooms. In the passage from Revelation, God is imaged as coming from heaven to make his dwelling place with us. It is imagery that is both grand and personal. His coming is with glory and majesty, but his presence among us is very personal, wiping away tears from the eyes of the fearful and the wretched. Whether the home be in heaven or on earth, it is the presence of a gentle and loving God that brings comfort and hope.

The "wiping away of tears" is a powerful image of comforting. Though it is hard to imagine a world in which there would be no reason to cry, we know what it is like to be comforted while we are crying. Is it possible that one could be so surrounded by loving care that needs are met the moment they arise? Eliminating all negativities from life, especially the negativity of death, strains the imagination to its limit, but such is our hope for when we will be at home with God.

Dwelling with God also invites imagery of human fulfillment. All of us dream about who we might someday be or what we might someday do. Those dreams often get smashed when we are brought up against the harsh realities of a world where competition is more characteristic of life together than cooperation. Dwelling with God, in whose image we were created, means that we can dream again, this time with confidence that we can become the kind of people that God intended us to be. So often death seems to cut short the time that we need to realize our dreams, to fulfill our ambitions, to achieve our goals. Far from being a place of passive complacency, when we are at home with God we will be able to live with a passion and an abandonment that we risk only on rare occasions in the here and now.

## Notes

1. Walter A. Hansen, ed., *Luther's Works,* vol. 4, *Lectures on Genesis Chapters 21–25* (St. Louis: Concordia Publishing House, 1965), p. 117.

2. Ibid, p. 119.

3. Ibid, p. 116.

# 3. Historical Shifts in the Images Used for Facing Death

The thesis of this chapter is that the expressions of faith Christians have used in facing death vary considerably from age to age, depending on the imagery of death in a particular period of history. We see that already in Scripture. Throughout most of the Old Testament there is little evidence of any anticipation of life after death, and thus little imagery of hope connected with such anticipation. By contrast, images of heaven abound in a Christian consciousness that is wrapped around the core of an Easter faith. An equally striking contrast in the imagery of death over time can be seen in the difference between images of the end of Israel as a covenant community (particularly strong in the exile) and the end of "little me" (particularly strong now). The emphasis throughout Scripture is on the fate of the community, though the fate of the individual becomes increasingly important in Christian reflections on the risen Christ.

Though the contrasts in the particular expressions of faith are often sharp, there is an amazing similarity in the content of the faith that produces the imagery. At the risk of oversimplification, I would describe the core of that content as an enduring hold on the trustable promise of the God of Abraham and the Father of our Lord Jesus Christ. No matter how the threat of death is experienced, the presence and power of God are always perceived as resources that can and do overcome that threat. To put it in a slightly different way, images of death and hope vary because death is perceived differently, not because God is perceived differently. God is always the God of promise, who can be counted on to be present with his power and love no matter what threat may loom on the horizon. Faith holds on to that promise, and images of comfort and hope flow out of that faith in a never-ending stream.

We turn now to a history of the imagery which Christians have used in their encounter with death since biblical times. This will not be a history of Christian thought for purposes of tracing the changing patterns of a theology of death. Instead the focus will be on the patterns of imagery which can be discerned as first-level reflections on the experience of death and dying.

Why should there be a chapter devoted to historical shifts in the church's use of imagery in facing death? There are three reasons. First, one ought always to ask what is frightening about death before providing reassuring images that may have little to do with that fear. Pastoral care always begins with diagnosis. Second, we should be aware of the rich resources of imagery in the church's tradition. Finally, awareness of historical diversity can provide a stimulus to a more creative use of our imagination in search of images of faith which the church can use in its pastoral care of those who are facing death in our own time.

We will use categories suggested by Philippe Ariès in his masterful historical study of *The Hour of Our Death*,[1] to distinguish four different ways in which death has been experienced in Western civilization. The first he calls "tamed death," an attitude of calmness and serenity in the face of death that characterizes almost the first thousand years of the Christian era. This was followed by a period that Aries calls "the death of the self," which has its origins in the seventh century, comes to full flower in the twelfth century, and comes to an end in the eighteenth century. This was an era in which a heightened sense of both individual identity and fear of judgment combined to make death a horror as it has never been before or since. The eighteenth and nineteenth centuries are characterized by attitudes formed around "the death of the other," a period marked both by a romanticizing of death and anguished feelings of grief. Aries calls the twentieth century a period of "forbidden death," an era marked by the absence of death awareness in a culture which has made death as taboo a subject as sexuality once was.

## Tamed Death

There was a strong expectation among early Christians that the end of the world was coming soon, probably within their lifetime. As that anticipation began to fade, a new question about life after death began to emerge. What happens between the time of death and the cosmic resurrection which comes at the end time? The early fathers of the church, most of them heavily influenced by Greek thought, turned naturally to

the Platonic doctrine of the immortality of the soul as a way to answer
this question, and they used it in such a matter-of-fact way that we must
consider it part of the classical way of understanding death from the very
beginning of the Christian era. There was no debate in the early church
between advocates of the soul's immortality and defenders of the resurrection. The fathers of the church defended the resurrection of the body
as a cosmic event at the end of time, but that was not viewed as a contradiction to the comforting belief that at the time of death the soul is
carried by angels to God himself in heaven. The immortality of the soul
was not a philosophical idea for early Christians, but an article of faith
useful for purposes of comforting those who are anguished by feelings
of loss.

There is relatively little speculation in the early church about the
fate of the soul in this interim period between death and resurrection.
Generally it is regarded as a period of inactivity with sleep as the most
common image to describe the state of body and soul as both await the
common hour of salvation, when all are raised and changed. It is a period
of history when death is perceived as tame, with little to fear in the sleep
of the dead. It is amazing that the images of death are so tame in this
early Christian era, dominated as it was by persecution and the threat of
violent death for anyone who admitted to being Christian. In spite of that
external threat, the images of faith are full of hope and confidence in the
future, and that is particularly true in the cult of the martyred saints
whose living and dying left such a profound impression on the piety of
the people of their time. It was through identification with the saints in
both life and death that the early Christians found the faith and the cour-
age to face their own dying. We turn now to some of the dominant images of faith in this early Christian era.


## *Eternal Rest, Refreshment, and Perpetual Light*

These three images often appear together in the literature and liturgy
of the early Christians, as for example in this ancient prayer for the dead:
"Give rest to the soul of your servant in a place of light, in a place of
refreshment, from which pain, distress and wailing have departed."[2]

Rest or sleep, the dominant image of the three, is found also in
Scripture. Jesus spoke of death as sleep in the stories of Lazarus (Jn
11:1–45) and the raising of the daughter of Jairus (Mk 5:22–43). St. Paul

speaks of those who have "fallen asleep in Christ" (1 Cor 15:18) and says that "through Jesus, God will bring with him those who have fallen asleep" (1 Thess 4:14). The author of Hebrews speaks of death as entering into the sabbath rest of God (4:1–11).

The biblical imagery of death as entering a period of peaceful sleep did not lose its soothing power until Christians began to anticipate purgatory rather than rest at the time of death. Along with his rejection of purgatory, Luther revived early Christian usage when he spoke of death as a "deep, untroubled sleep" and the grave as a "bed of repose." It is imagery which is still meaningful, though it feeds superstition as well as faith. Bodies are placed in caskets as if they were sleeping, and people usually speak only in subdued tones around the corpse as if they feared "waking the dead." Rituals of communication with the dead (visits to the cemetery, placing flowers on the grave, addressing the dead at the burial site) imply a felt sense that they are really there, but asleep.

One feels refreshed after a night's sleep, and so the images of sleep and refreshment belong together. To people who live in a climate in which a pitiless sun withers the vegetation and turns the land into a burning desert, refreshment meant a green oasis around a water hole where the exhausted traveler can be refreshed and regain his strength. The imagery would suggest that the gates of death do not open to a vast wasteland, but rather to green pastures and still waters. Led there by the good shepherd, one's soul will be restored.

Light is one of the deepest longings which human beings experience, darkness being a symbol of chaos (prior to creation) and death (at Calvary). The psalms speak of the light that radiates from the face of God: "Lift up the light of thy countenance upon us, O Lord" (4:6). The identification of darkness with death and light with God's presence is common throughout Scripture and culminates in the Book of Revelation with the imagery of heaven. "And night shall be no more; they need no light of lamp or sun, for the Lord God will be their light, and they shall reign for ever and ever" (22:5).

Well publicized accounts of near-death experiences suggest that light is a natural and possibly universal image of hope in the midst of dying. Imagery of light, as well as rest and refreshment, will be utilized in the guided imagery exercises to provide the same kind of comfort and ease that it obviously gave to the early Christians.

## Death as Birth

It is from the era of the martyred saints that we get the image of death as birth. The joy of early Christians at the birth of a child was tempered by the doctrine of original sin. The good news was God's gift of new life; the bad news was the inheritance of sin that came with the gift. There was no such ambiguity about the day of death, according to Chrysostom, especially if it was the death of a martyr, "for death is also a birth and a better birth than the birth into this life."[3] Using the same imagery as Chrysostom, Ignatius anticipates his martyrdom with these words: "The pains of birth are upon me." When he heard that some of his supporters were attempting to prevent him from being martyred, he said: "Suffer me, my brethren; hinder me not from living."[4]

It was common to speak of the day of death as "dies natalis" (day of birth). Inscriptions on the tomb of martyrs indicated the day of their martyrdom as their birthday. Often the tomb of an ordinary Christian would have the inscription that the person died on the *dies natalis* of such and such martyr, a sure sign of hope in the intercession of that martyr. To die is to be born into a life of unambiguous joy and peace.

## The Tomb of the Saint as a Door to Paradise

There was strong motivation among early Christians to be buried *ad sanctos,* near the martyred saints who, according to Tertullian, had the sole key to paradise. Countless inscriptions from the sixth to the eighth centuries repeat the same set phrases: "who deserved to be associated with the sepulchers of the saints," "resting in peace and in the company of the martyrs," "laid to rest *ad sanctos.*"

Initially the martyrs were buried outside the cities. Basilicas were built on the sites of revered tombs to accommodate the visit of pilgrims and to serve as the residence for the dead, the basilica becoming the nucleus of a cemetery *ad sanctos* to secure the protection of the martyred saint. Soon tombs invaded the interiors of churches, beginning with the cemeterial basilicas, and that in spite of the consistent canonical prohibitions against the practice. Already by the fourth and fifth centuries the churches of Roman Africa were at least partially paved with mosaic tombs which bore epitaphs and pictures of the deceased. The customary procedure from then until the eighteenth century was burial inside the churches, which were veritable cities of the dead with wall-to-wall tombs, bones placed in niches in the walls, mass burials around the apse in the atrium, and charnel houses to contain the bones of decomposed corpses. "The cemetery is the holy dormitory of the dead and, according to Honorius of Autun, the bosom of the Church, the *ecclesiae gremium,* where she rekindles the souls of those who are dead in body to restore them to eternal life, just as by baptism she revives the dead who are still in this world."[5]

The tomb of the saint was a door to paradise because, as Peter Brown suggests, each of the martyred saints was held to be a point where heaven and earth were joined. They were the living dead, "dead" to the world while alive and radiating life in their death. Healings were common at the shrines of the saints, especially on the festival day of their birth—not their birth into this life, but their death-birth into the life of paradise.

We live in an age of space consciousness, an age when the distance between heaven and earth seems greater with each new discovery of the vastness of space. What the early Christians had in the image of a martyred saint, who was both dead and alive at the same time, was an intimate friend and constant companion who bridged the barrier between this life and the next as naturally as a friend from another country can bridge the barrier between two nations. That experience can never be ours, but with the use of guided imagery we can have access to wisdom figures who have shaped our identity and continue to be important in our lives even though they have long since passed through the door between this life and the next.

## Death of the Self

Near the turn of the seventh century there was a shift in the way death was imaged. The theme of judgment assumed a prominence in the Latin church that would have a profound influence on the way Christians understood death for the next one thousand years. Aries calls this the period of "the death of the self" because individual awareness of one's own death became prominent during this period. The combination of judgment and a growing individualism evoked a fear of death which reached an intensity unequaled in any age before or since.

The fear of judgment finds expression in the doctrine of purgatory, which has its beginnings in the pastoral theology of Pope Gregory the Great (about 600 A.D.) and comes into full flower by the thirteenth century. The purging value of suffering both in this life and in purgatory was supported by Anselm's doctrine of the atonement, which emphasized God's justice and his demand for full satisfaction for sin. This not only laid a foundation for the doctrine of penance but helped create a new desire for knowledge of self. It also facilitated a shift in emphasis from cosmic to individual salvation. The judgment of God became an individual matter settled at the hour of death. Thomas Aquinas argued that since both reward and punishment flow from the soul to the body and not the other way around, there is no reason why souls should wait for a reunion with their bodies to get on with the business of enduring the punishment which was God's judgment at the hour of death. And so we have a theology in place which supports the practice of indulgences and Masses for the dead literally all the way to the end time.

What brought comfort to those who so feared the wrath of God? A good death and guarantees of eternity. Since judgment occurred at the moment of death, the way one died became very important. A whole new genre of literature on the art of dying emerged in the Middle Ages, treatises on the techniques of dying well. Guarantees of eternity also brought comfort to the troubled souls of this fearful age. The fires of purgatory fueled the need of people to protect themselves and others from the consuming judgment of God. Masses for the dead were said continuously in a great many chapels or monastery churches after the ninth century. At Cluny, these Masses went on day and night. The greatest security of all was gained through a perpetual endowment for Masses, which could be ensured by funding a chapel with the provision that a Mass for the donor would be said there every day or at least every year in perpetuity.

Images of death are to be found everywhere in this period of history where people were preoccupied with the fate of their individual souls and the overwhelming fear of judgment. They appear in art, in literature, in liturgy, in music, in tomb effigies, in sculptures. The images are products of tortured imaginations. They are designed to evoke fear rather than comfort or hope, fear of the hour of death and the individual judgment that awaits each person in that dread event, fear of the purifying fires of purgatory, fear of the last judgment that awaits us all at the end of time, and fear of hell if you have not lived well. Gone are the images of rest and refreshment which are so common in the early Christian era, not because Christians in this period are more sadistic or masochistic (though some of the imagery borders on that), but because fear was believed to be the most effective way to encourage the moral life, a life that could stand the test of judgment. A brief description of some of the most prominent imagery in this period is provided in the following paragraphs.

## The Dance of Death

The hightening of death consciousness in the Middle Ages was epitomized in the call of *memento mori* (remember death). The imagery of the Dance of Death sounded that theme to every corner of Western Christendom by allowing the dead to enter the world of the living, reminding them that they are but a breath away from the realm of the dead.

The most famous depiction of The Dance of Death was a painting on the wall of the churchyard of the Church of the Innocents in Paris in the fifteenth century. This famous churchyard was the burial ground of thousands in Paris who were interred in mass graves and whose bones were later placed in charnel houses erected around the churchyard. This was the setting for the first artistic representation of a procession or a dance that joined the living and the dead. Aries provides a good description of the imagery of the dance:

> The danse macabre is an eternal round in which the dead alternate with the living. The dead lead the dance; indeed, they are the only ones dancing. Each couple consists of a naked mummy, rotting, sexless, and highly animated, and a man or woman, dressed according to his or her social condition and paralyzed by surprise. Death holds out its hand to the living person whom it will draw along with it, but who has not yet obeyed the summons. The art lies in the contrast between the rhythm of the dead and the rigidity of the living. The moral purpose was to remind the viewer both of the uncertainty of the hour of death and of the equality of all people in face of death.[6]

## The Fateful Hour of Death

Since a person's eternal destiny was determined by the attitude and faith displayed in the final hours of life, it is not surprising that images of dying are abundant in this period. In the popular imagination the separation of the soul from the body appeared as a most painful process similar to the uprooting of a tree from the soil to which it is bound by a multitude of roots. The departing soul, often depicted in the form of a small child exiting from the mouth of the dying person, was at that moment frightfully vulnerable to the host of devils waiting to seize the soul and carry it off to the confines of eternal hell. The dying person could expect to see and hear devils on every side, making ugly faces and horrible noises. In the mystery plays of the fifteenth and sixteenth centuries the deathbed was depicted as the great battlefield where one's enemy, the devil, drew up all his strongest forces for one final and brutal assault. Every temptation to which the soul had been subjected in the long days of its pilgrimage on earth was arrayed against it.

Two images which contributed to this sense of judgment at the hour of death were the weighing of the souls of the dead and the book of life. Each life ends up on the scales of justice at the end of life, and angels are leaning over the balconies of heaven to witness the outcome. A concern for justice also informs the imagery of the book of life, which was originally a book of the elect. In this period it becomes the book of the damned. At the end of the Middle Ages the accounts in the book of life are kept by those who profit from them, the devils, who are confident that the evil will outweigh the good. A haunting fear of the dying person was to imagine that "his guardian angel, distressed, abandons him, dropping his book. All the good works that were recorded in it have been erased, because everything good he has done is without merit in the eyes of heaven. To the left, we see the devil presenting him with a book that contains the whole *history* of his evil life."[7]

## *Purgatory*

The most vivid imagery of purgatory in the Middle Ages can be found in Dante's *Inferno*. Why did it become so popular? People experienced such high levels of anxiety about the state of their souls at the time of death that images of rest and refreshment were either unreal or premature. Images of purifying fire were more immediate and even more gratifying. Better to be deposited by an angel for a final purging of the soul than to take the chance that one's soul might be snatched by the evil one for an eternity of hell.

The following quotation from *The Craft of Dying* is an example of the actual imagery used:

Now farewell, fellows and friends most dear: for now in my passing
I cast the eyes of my mind into purgatory, whether that I shall now
be led, and out thereof I shall not pass till I have yielded the last far-
thing of my debt for sin. There I behold with the eye of mine heart
wretchedness and sorrow, and manifold pain and tormenting. Alas,
my wretched! There I see—among other pains that belong to that
place—rising up flames of fire, and the souls of the wretched fold cast
therein; up and down, to and fro, that run as sparks of fire in midst
of that burning fire: right as in a great town, all one fire. And in the
fire and in the smoke the sparks be borne up and down. So the souls,
lamenting for sorrow of their pains, cry everyone and say these
words: Have mercy on me, have mercy on me, at the last, yet that be
my friends."[8]

## Death of the Other

A new attitude toward death emerges after the Enlightenment. What
was fearful about death was no longer the prospect of judgment at the
time of death but the physical separation from the deceased. Preoccu-
pation with the beloved has long been recognized as characteristic of the
literature of Romanticism, but it is characteristic as well of the imagery
of death in this period.

Death has started to hide in this period; by mid-twentieth century it
is almost completely hidden. In the nineteenth century it conceals itself
under a mask of beauty. The "death is beautiful" motif can be seen in
funerary art, in tombs and monuments, in cemeteries like Mt. Audubun
and later Forest Lawn, and in syrupy-sweet liturgies. But beauty could
not be associated with death if it had not ceased to be associated with sin
and the judgment of God. For the pious believers of the nineteenth century, and the twentieth century as well, hell is a dogma that is memorized
in catechism but foreign to their experience.

If hell is gone, heaven has changed too. The next world becomes
the scene of the reunion of those who have been separated by death, a
separation that the living found it impossible to accept. There is a great
outpouring of emotion both prior to and at the point of the final separation. Agnostics cultivate the memory of the dead with an emotional
intensity that creates as vivid an impression of their continued existence
as the faith of believers. Cemeteries, no longer linked to the church, be-

come places to visit in the practice of what Aries calls "the cult of the dead." The desire to communicate with the dead gave rise to spiritualism and the sense that loved ones who have died are somehow present to the extrasensory experience of the living.

Accounts of deathbed scenes and celestial communications crowded the bookstalls in the decades before and after the Civil War. This consolation literature stressed the importance of dying and caring for the dead. It encouraged elaborate funerary practices, conspicuous methods of burial and commemoration, and careful attention to vision of the afterlife.

It was not unusual for the grieving to spend large portions of time at the rural cemeteries which became popular in this period and are another example of the romanticizing of death in nineteenth century America. These planned and picturesque rural cemeteries had paths with pastoral names, gentle rills, green slopes, and newly popular graveside flowers that were meant to flatter the idealized but docile deceased. The severe tombstones of the eighteenth century, with images of a hollow-eyed death's head or an hourglass, gave way to more gentle images of angels, birds, flowers, cinerary urns, and weeping willows, all pointing to the beauties of a heavenly paradise.

Gone from this period are the images of judgment and terror: souls of the newly dead snatched by devils and dragged into the fires of hell, dancing figures of death among the living, death's heads on tombstones, death crowned as a king or depicted in a triumphal procession. In its place are images which evoke feelings of peace and beauty: a lovely rural cemetery, quiet conversations with the dead at the graveside, solid steel caskets bedecked with flowers, lifelike corpses in funeral parlors for people to "view," emotional displays of an outpouring of grief, the depiction of heaven as our home. We will limit ourselves to an examination of one of these images, heaven as our home, an image which is not only representative of this period but compelling to Christians in every age.

## Heaven as Our Home

It is Jesus who gives us the first imagery of heaven as a home: "In my Father's house are many rooms; if it were not so, would I have told you that I go to prepare a place for you? And when I go and prepare a place for you, I will come again and will take you to myself, that where

I am you may be also'' (Jn 14:2–3). The setting for these words was the last supper. Jesus was preparing his disciples for his departure and attempting to calm their troubled hearts by imaging for them a time and place beyond this present crisis where they will be with him in his Father's house.

For most people home is associated with security, warmth, love, good food, and good people. It's a place where you can always be sure that you will be welcome, no matter how bad you feel about yourself as a person or how down you are on your luck. Home is usually ''back home'' to the imagination. We think of times that we returned home after being gone for a long period of time, especially the first time. We think of holiday meals and cozy, warm evenings around the fire. Of course, home wasn't always like that. But to the imagination the thought of going ''back home'' is likely to evoke the positive feelings associated with having a place, a secure place, to be and to become.

Jesus takes this image of home out of the past and places it in the future. Instead of looking back to a time and place in the past that was secure in times of crisis, Jesus invites us to look beyond all the crises which may lie in front of us to a home, his Father's home, where he beckons us to join him and share in a life which is more joyous and fulfilling than the happiest of our family days.

The imagery of heaven as home can be sentimentalized, as it often was in the consolation literature of the nineteenth century, but that ought not to deter us from its use today. So many of our yearnings for human fulfillment are intertwined with the lives of parents, brothers, sisters, spouse, and children. If home served as a haven for us on storm-tossed days of our life on earth, what more appropriate image for what we yearn for in heaven?

## Invisible Death

The fourth historical period is the modern one, characterized by Aries as ''Invisible Death.'' As noted in the first chapter, death has been a taboo topic until very recently in our century. In an age of death-denial, the imagery of death is hidden but powerful. Ernst Becker's **Denial of Death** is an analysis of images of terror deep within the unconscious, images so frightening that a lifetime is spent in building defenses against them. Rather than focus on imagery buried within the psyche, we will focus on two images of death which are unique to our time and available for public scrutiny.

## A Prolonged Death

The massive technology of modern medicine has been employed in countless ways to prolong the lives of people in life-threatening situations. Because that technology must be located in a hospital, almost everyone who is seriously ill is taken to a hospital, making a hospital the most likely place for a person to die. This life-extending technology brings hope to people in periods of crisis and is responsible for extending the lives of people who would otherwise certainly have died. The respirator, which supplies artificial support for breathing, has become the symbol for all such technology.

Prolonging life easily shades into prolonging death. It is a source of considerable distress for many people to imagine themselves being kept alive on a respirator when there is no reasonable hope for recovery. Stories of the courtroom battle between parents and physicians over the fate of Karen Ann Quinlan have burned an image of meaningless lingering death on the minds of a great many Americans, prompting public support for living wills and the right to die.

Hospice has countered the imagery of meaningless, lingering death with an image of dying in relative comfort, surrounded by people who are loving and caring. A number of the exercises in Part II foster an imagery of death like that of Hospice.

## Images of Mass Destruction

The most haunting images of death in the modern era are images of mass destruction. The mushroom cloud billowing up into the sky is an image of almost unimaginable destruction. What makes it so difficult to imagine is its massiveness and its psychological distance. Movies like "The Day After" have helped to bring the reality closer to home, but most people block out the imagery of mass death from their minds most of the time. It is different in European countries where the threat is nearer and the memories of war more vivid. The future of the race may depend on our ability to keep the terror of those images strong in the minds and hearts of those who must make decisions about the use of those weapons.

Images of mass death are not new. In the Middle Ages the plague wiped out nearly a third of the population of Western Europe. Whole families were decimated when the illness struck. The difference then was that death was like an external threat over which nobody had control, much the way tornadoes or earthquakes are today. The mass destruction of the modern era comes by means of human action. Nuclear destruction is a human invention and thus subject to human control.

Talking abstractly about nuclear destruction is different from vicariously experiencing it by means of a movie or guided imagery. Dare one intentionally provoke the high anxiety which is inevitably generated by such an experience? The promoters of ''The Day After'' answered in the affirmative. There is no exercise in guided imagery on nuclear destruction in this volume, though I seriously considered including one. Though imagining oneself in a nuclear holocaust is a good and even necessary exercise if we are to survive, some measure of detachment is also needed. Guided imagery would not permit the detachment and for many would be counter productive.

### Notes

1. Philippe Ariès, *The Hour of Our Death,* trans. Helen Weaver (N.Y.: Alfred A Knopf, 1981).
2. Achille M. Triacca, ed., *The Temple of the Holy Spirit: Sickness and Death of the Christian in the Liturgy* (N.Y.: Pueblo Press, 1975), p. 25.
3. Alfred C. Rush, *Death and Burial in Christian Antiquity* (Catholic University Press, 1941), p. 80.
4. Ibid, p. 77.
5. Ariès, p. 42.
6. Ibid, p. 116.
7. Ibid, p. 105.
8. Frances M. Comper, ed., *The Book of the Craft of Dying* (N.Y.: Longmans, Green & Co., 1917), pp. 118f.

# 4. Liturgical Imagery for Facing Death

The liturgy is a natural place for us to go in search of images which express the faith and hope of the Christian community in its ministry to the dying and bereaved. While doctrinal language is the language of the intellect, the liturgy—like the Bible—speaks with a language full of rich imagery. We will be examining the imagery of liturgical language as it is used in three different settings. We look first at the rites of the church which are most closely associated with death and dying: Easter vigil, baptism, and funeral liturgy. Our primary focus will be on the imagery of paschal faith, which is at the heart of the church's theology of death and dying. Hymnody is a second source of liturgical imagery which reflects the church's paschal faith. The rituals of pastoral care which are used in a ministry to the dying and the bereaved are a third source of liturgical imagery.

The liturgy celebrates both beginnings and endings and considers both to be occasions for the gracious activity of God. The baptismal liturgy marks the beginning of life and the funeral liturgy marks the ending—both linked inseparably together in meaning and action. To be baptized is to share in the death and resurrection of Christ, apart from which baptism would have no more power than a ritual which celebrates the coming of spring after a cold and lifeless winter. There is no escape from the fear of death for any human being, but baptismal faith fastens on to the promise that there is no end to the relationship with God which has its beginning in the baptismal waters of immortality. Though human life has an ending, life with God does not.

The same kind of close linkage between beginnings and endings ought to characterize the funeral liturgy. If death is at the center of the baptismal liturgy, then baptism ought to be at the center of the funeral liturgy. Endings and beginnings are deeply intertwined in the gracious action of God who puts an end to the power of sin and death at the very beginning and promises resurrection and new beginnings at the very end.

That's why we go back to the beginning when we come to the ending, why the beginning and the ending are so closely linked. The promise given us when we were helpless infants is the promise which sustains us when we are helpless in our dying and helpless in our grieving. It is the promise of a God who knows the helplessness of beginnings and endings, birth and death, for he was present in the infant suckling at the breast of Mary and in the young man gasping life's last breath upon a cross. It is the promise of a God whose power is revealed in weakness, whose victory is achieved in defeat, whose life emerges phoenix-like from death. It is the promise of a God who holds us as securely at our end as in our beginning.

## The Paschal Mystery as Resource
## for Encountering Death

The beginnings and endings are held together by the paschal mystery, which provides the context of meaning within the liturgy for understanding all of life, but particularly the harsh realities of death and dying. By paschal mystery we mean the mysterious depths of meaning in the death and resurrection of Jesus. To affirm that the Christian life is rooted in the death and resurrection of Jesus Christ is the strongest affirmation of faith that can be made in confronting death. Liturgy proclaims, celebrates, and nourishes that paschal faith. It is incorporation into the paschal mystery that constitutes the making of a Christian in baptism. It is the paschal mystery actualized in the bread and wine of the Eucharist that sustains the life of faith. And it is the final reenactment of the paschal mystery in the funeral liturgy which assures us that the life of faith which began in baptism and was nourished by the Eucharist will not end with death but find fulfillment in the eternal presence of Jesus.

The primary places where death is encountered in the liturgy are baptism, the paschal cycle (and especially the Easter vigil), the funeral service, Scripture readings, preaching (when based on assigned pericopes), and hymnody. All of these liturgical resources draw on imagery from the paschal mystery to express the meaning of faith in its encounter with death. Remove the paschal mystery from the liturgy and there is no suitable language for dealing with death. One could make the same statement about Scripture, of course, but the statement is more obvious in relation to the liturgy because liturgy links the word and action of God to our daily experience of living and dying.

Paschal imagery is the imagery of passage. St. Augustine comments that "a certain passage from death to life has been consecrated in the passion and resurrection of the Lord." The liturgy enables us to make that passage our own. Whether it be baptism, the Easter vigil, or the funeral, the liturgy is an enactment of the passage from death to life, from darkness to light, from bondage to freedom, from despair to hope.[1]

Images of passage have always been at the center of liturgies that have to do with death and dying. We find this ancient prayer for safe passage in the Gelasian Sacramentary: "Allow his spirit to pass by the gates of hell and the paths of darkness and to abide in the dwellings of saints and in the holy light you once promised to Abraham and his posterity." The "dwelling of the saints" to which the dead go is imaged in a variety of ways: eternal dwelling, heavenly Jerusalem, place of light, place of refreshment, abode of rest, bosom of Abraham. "Let him be acknowledged by your own and in your merciful goodness let him be carried to the place of refreshment and repose in the bosom of Abraham."

The primary source for the imagery of passage comes from Scripture, and the liturgy makes rich use of it. In the Old Testament it is the passage of Israel from bondage in Egypt through the wilderness to the promised land. We are invited to identify with a pilgrim people whose faith is tested by watery chaos and wilderness wandering until they receive the inheritance that has been promised them. In the New Testament it is the passage of Christ through life and death to life eternal. Jesus is the suffering servant whose passage through both life and death opens up a path to fullness of life for all who make his pilgrimage their own.

We turn now to the Easter vigil, the most ancient of all liturgies, the ritual reenactment of Christ's passage from death to life, the setting for all baptisms in the early church, and a primary source of imagery for understanding the paschal mystery.

## The Easter Vigil

The people of Israel were bound to keep holy the night of the Passover each year by a vigil of prayer and praise. "This is the night for keeping vigil in the Lord's honor, this night when he brought them forth out of the land of Egypt; this night all the children of Israel must observe in every generation" (Ex 12:42). Jesus kept that vigil with his disciples on the *night* before his passion; he died on Calvary while there was *darkness* over the earth, and he rose from the dead in the darkness of the *night* that followed the paschal sabbath, for "it was still dark" (Jn 20:1) when Mary Magdalene found the sepulcher empty. It is not surprising that the first Christians, still rooted deeply in Jewish traditions, felt bound to keep the holy night of the resurrection by a vigil in honor of the Lord of the new covenant even as they had before kept holy the night of the exodus, the supreme symbol of the old covenant.

Like the vigil of the Passover, the Easter vigil is a night for both memory and anticipation. Memory reaches back to the first Passover for images to express the meaning of the second: "For this indeed is the paschal feast in which the true Lamb is slain, by whose blood the doorposts of the faithful are made holy." Memory relives the passage through death and hell: "This is the night in which, breaking the chains of death, Christ arises from hell in triumph." Memory recalls a darkness that could not contain the light: "This is the night of which it is written: 'and the night is as clear as the day'; and, 'then shall my night be turned into day.' " It is a night for remembering the mystery of Christ passing through the darkness of death and hell and bursting forth in the light of the resurrection.

The vigil is also a night of anticipation, not waiting "for the Lord to arise," as Augustine said in a homily for the vigil, but rather "waiting for the return of the Lord, waiting 'until he comes.' " We await the risen Christ, whose coming in glory actually began that first Easter night. And when will he come? Lactantius (about 310) suggests that it will be on the very night of the vigil, for on this night the door to heaven is ajar.

Between the remembering of Christ's passage from death to life and the anticipation of our passage from this life to the kingdom of heaven is the present moment of the vigil itself and the sacramental enactment of the passage from death to life in those who are being baptized in this most holy of all nights. Already before the third century it had gradually become the custom throughout the church to choose this time before any other for initiating new members into the church. From the fourth century baptism in the Easter vigil was the standard practice. St. Basil says: "What time is more appropriate for baptism than this day of the pasch? It is the memorial day of the resurrection. Baptism implants in us the seed of resurrection. Let us then receive the grace of resurrection on the day of the resurrection."[2]

Paschal imagery is appropriate for both the vigil and the baptismal ritual which is deeply embedded within it, as is clear from this homily of Cyril of Jerusalem for those who had been baptized at the vigil:

> After these things (stripping and anointing) you were led to the holy pool of sacred baptism, just as Christ was carried from the cross to the tomb which is before our eyes. And after each of you was asked whether he believed in the name of the Father, and of the Son, and of the Holy Spirit, you made that saving profession, descended three times into the water, and ascended again, thus suggesting signifying symbolically the three day burial of Christ. For as the saviour spent three days and three nights in the heart of the earth, so you also, in your first emersion from the water, enacted the first day Christ spent in the earth, and by your immersion, the night: Just as at night one no longer sees very well, and in the daytime is surrounded by light, so in immersion, as at night, you saw nothing, but at emersion were, so to speak, in daylight. And at that very moment you were both dying and being born, for the water of salvation was at once your grave and mother. And what Solomon spoke of others applies to you as well. He declared, "There is a time to be born and a time to die" (Eccl 3:2); conversely, for you there was a time to die and a time to be born. This happened simultaneously, and your birth went hand in hand with your death.[3]

Cyril's reference to "the tomb which is before our eyes" is to be taken quite literally since he is speaking in the Constantinian basilica of the Holy Sepulcher, which was built on what was concluded to be the tomb of the Savior. To speak of the water of salvation as both grave and mother is to capture the deepest meaning of baptism as both death and birth, ending and beginning. Water is closely associated with both death and deliverance from death. Israel saw in unruly waters the image of pre-creation chaos and a symbol of the powers that threatened God's sovereignty. Yet Israel could go through the "deep waters" in the confidence that Yahweh is Lord over the deep. Stories of the exodus and Jonah offer reassurance that in time of threat God can be counted on "to draw me out of many waters" (Ps 18:16). Even as the cross is an image not only of death, but of the death of death, so the water of baptism is an image of both grave and womb. "The font is a sort of sepulcher," says St. Ambrose. But more than sepulcher! "O Womb! Who daily brings forth without sorrow sons for the kingdom of heaven." Baptism as grave and mother—powerful imagery for both beginnings and endings.

## The Funeral Liturgy as Passage from Death to Life

Mark Twain once said: "A community may be known by the funerals it holds." Some funerals try to cover up grief and the reality of death with eulogies of high praise, huge displays of flowers, and a natural looking corpse. Other funerals are designed to facilitate grief since that is regarded as the primary purpose of the funeral. Still others hold memorial services instead of funerals as occasions for family and friends to remember the deceased and all that she meant to them.

If the historic liturgy of the church is our guide, the funerals we hold are to be Passovers of human death, Passovers made authentic in union with Jesus Christ, dead and risen. The Passover of our Lord is at the center of all history, and in the Christian rites of passage, especially baptism and the funeral, we need to be reminded that our destiny is firmly rooted in that event. Mark Bangert suggests that the Easter vigil can be our guide in understanding the dynamics of the funeral liturgy. Death, he says,

> is a personalized pasch, an Easter Vigil with new scenery, a variation on a theme composed from eternity! As personalized Easter Vigil, we can expect of death those same dynamics we have come to know in the death of the Lamb: the awful positing that darkness will prevail, the chilling confrontation with the chasm that has separated God and people (the brokenness of humanity beginning with Adam and Eve, the ascendency of chaos over light), the graceful persistence of light, victory, hope, and life, the assurance of sin forgiven, the pain of passage, and the total reliance on the power of God.[4]

The paschal theme is dominant in the earliest source we have for an actual funeral rite, the *Ordo Romanus 49,* a ritual which dates back to the eighth and perhaps to the seventh century. After the giving of the Viaticum (Eucharist for the dying), there follows the reading of the passion until death intervenes. Then follows the reading of the paschal Psalm 114 ("When Israel went forth from Egypt"). Following the ceremonial washing of the body, the remainder of the rite consists essentially of the procession from the place of death to the place of burial.

This procession features the chanting of a number of psalms and antiphons, among them the *In paradisum* "May the angels lead you into the paradise of God. May the martyrs welcome you at your coming. And may they lead you into the holy city Jerusalem." The procession is clearly an enactment of passage, a liturgical celebration of Christian death as participation in the paschal mystery. There is only a brief stop at the church for what later becomes a full blown funeral service, before the procession continues to the place of burial.

In contrast to the paschal celebration of earlier Christians, the rites of the dead used in the medieval church were marked by dread of death and fear of judgment. Gone was the living paschal faith that confidently believes in eternal life through the death and resurrection of Christ, and in its place came a fearful eschatology of the individual that is reflected in the twelfth century responsory called the *Libera:*

> Deliver me, Lord, from everlasting death in that awful day, when the heavens and the earth shall be moved, when you will come to judge the world by fire. Dread and trembling have laid hold upon me, and I fear exceedingly because of the judgment and the wrath to come. O that day, that day of wrath, of sore distress and of all wretchedness, that great and exceeding bitter day, when you will come to judge the world by fire.[5]

The funeral liturgy today is once again viewed as a celebration of the deceased's personal Passover from the power of sin and death and an anticipation in hope of entrance into the fullness of Christ's kingdom. The words from the Lutheran order of *The Commendation of the Dying* suggest the beginning of a journey: "May you return to the one who formed us out of the dust of the earth. Surrounded by the angels and triumphant saints, may Christ come to meet you as you go forth from this life." The journey begins with the commendation of the dying and ends at the cemetery, as Gordon Lathrop suggests in the following passage:

> We do the whole funeral procession from the house, to the church, to the cemetery, as if it is a journey—as if the dead are going somewhere! The procession, the movement, the assembly is the pilgrim people who believe *themselves* to be going somewhere, seeing it now and greeting it from afar. . . . The whole procession is only true if it

speaks of Christ. The cross at the head of it means to say that this is about the *transitus* of Jesus Christ, whose bursting of death to become something we can hardly name transfigures the whole event and makes going somewhere mean something.[6]

The funeral "journey" ends at the cemetery, the name given the place of burial by early Christians. Originally it meant a "sleeping place" or "dormitory." That fits well with the early Christian view of death as but a sleep consecrated by expectation of the promised awakening by Christ at his coming in glory.

And after the grave, then what? We can approach this final portal in the paschal procession with the deceased, but we can go no further—at least, not yet. For seeing what lies beyond this point we are wholly dependent on our imaginations. The imagination of a paschal faith can be trusted to produce images like those produced by the biblical writers and church fathers, some of which we referred to in the last two chapters. The reason those images can be trusted is because they are rooted in experience and not products of fantasy. The Christian's experience of heaven does not begin after the Christian has gone through the gates of death, but is an extension of the longing, the love, and the fullness of our present experience. The experiences of grace in our existence are centering points for our experience of heaven. We can look for images of heaven in the recollection of those moments when we felt close to God—perhaps in a moment of intimacy with another, or gripped by the grandeur of an awesome cathedral, or entranced by the majesty of a mountain. On such occasions we know something of ultimate reality, know that the longings of our heart will one day have their fulfillment. There are moments when we sense a mystery that we can enter into while at the same time realizing that we do not begin to fathom its depths, a mystery that transcends the heights and overshadows everything, a mystery that is hidden in the depths of all that is and extends beyond the deepest recesses of the real.

The imagination is given an opportunity to soar when reflecting in anticipation on the fullness of being which we see now only through a glass darkly, but will one day experience as a daily fulfillment of our deepest yearnings. The exercise in Chapter 9 entitled "Beyond the Gates of Death" is designed to facilitate the use of creative images to anticipate the completion of our humanity which awaits us beyond the grave.

## Hymnody

Hymnody contains a treasure-trove of images which express the church's faith and hope in relation to death. Though the hymnody of any denomination could be used to explore the richness of this imagery, I will limit myself to hymns found in the current *Lutheran Book of Worship*.[7] Hymnody gives free and full expression to the emotions of fear, longing, trust, sorrow, and joy. Images are particularly powerful tools for expressing the feeling as well as the meaning of faith. Thus it is not surprising that we should find ready use of imagery in the hymns of the church. It becomes even less surprising when one considers that so many of our hymns are occasioned by the Christian's encounter with death: baptisms, funerals, Lent, Holy Week, and Easter.

In hymnody death is imaged in an almost totally negative way (grim, dark, an enemy, an iron chain, a dark prison, gloomy halls, a dark vale, a dread angel), though on rare occasions it is depicted as "kind and gentle," "waiting to hush our final breath." The negativities of death, however, are almost always expressed within the framework of the Gospel and Christ's victory over death. Death can be imaged in all of its fierceness because the comfort of the Gospel offers assurance that the fierceness is like that of a caged lion. Since the images of death and the comfort of the Gospel are always found in such close conjunction in hymns, we will examine each in relation to the other.


## PASSAGE
### Fear: Wilderness  ◇  Comfort: Promised Land

It is appropriate that we begin with the dominant image of all liturgy, the image of passage through death to life. Israel's deliverance from bondage, its wilderness journey, and its entrance into Canaan are sources of imagery to depict the passage from death to life in baptism and at the end of life. Two examples will suffice:

> When I tread the verge of Jordan,
> Bid my anxious fears subside;
> Death of death and hell's destruction,
> Land me safe on Canaan's side. (343:3)

Though nature's strength decay, and earth and hell withstand,
To Canaan's bounds I urge my way at his command.
The watery deep I pass, with Jesus in my view,
And through the howling wilderness my way pursue.

The goodly land I see, with peace and plenty blest;
A land of sacred liberty, and endless rest.
There milk and honey flow, and oil and wine abound,
And trees of life forever grow with mercy crowned. (544:5–6)

Explicitly paschal images are, of course, abundant in the hymns written especially for Holy Week worship. The "day of resurrection . . . is the Passover of gladness . . . from death to life eternal" (141:1). So also "His blood now marks our door; faith points to it, death passes o'er" (134:3) and "Where the paschal blood is poured death's dread angel sheathes the sword" (210:3).

The sacred memory of Passover in the history of both Israel and Jesus is the major but not the only source of imagery for depicting the passage of the Christian from this life to the next, as these verses show:

Lord, when the shadows lengthen and night has come,
I know that you will strengthen my steps toward home,
And nothing can impede me, O blessed Friend!
So take my hand and lead me unto the end. (333:3)

In weakness be thy love my pow'r
And when the storms of life shall cease,
O Jesus, in that final hour
Be thou my rod and staff and guide
And draw me safely to thy side! (336:4)

Imagery of life as a journey and death as a homecoming is common. Death is depicted as "that final journey" (161:5) or "our homeward pathway" (157:5). It is the home of the Lord of life (289:3), which is "our true home" (317:4). The savior's call summons me homeward (485:4), and the angels, "messengers of love," are sent to bring me home (266:6; 325:3).

If heaven is our home, one must go through the door of death to get there. This door is imaged in both negative and positive ways, depending on what one expects on the other side. If I fear the judgment of God, then with "trembling breath" do "I pass its gloomy portal" (133:5), which is also called "the tomb's dark portal" (132:5). However, the "bars from heaven's high portals" have fallen as a result of Christ's victory over death (135:4). For the Christian the gate of death opens to heaven, not hell. By his death Christ "has opened heaven's door" (55:2), and the gates of death hold no more terror. Indeed, "He brings me to the portal that leads to bliss untold" (129:6).

The hymnody of the church draws freely on this imagery of water, which symbolizes both chaos and life-giving power. The following hymn, written by Luther, is a good example:

> Even as we live each day, death our life embraces.
> Who is there to bring us help, rich, forgiving graces?
> You only, Lord, you only!
> Baptized in Christ's life-giving flood:
> Water and his precious blood—
> Holy and righteous God, holy and mighty God,
> Holy and all-merciful Savior, everlasting God,
> By grace bring us safely through the flood of bitter death.
> Lord, have mercy. (350)

"Bring us safely through the flood of bitter death" is juxtaposed with "baptized in Christ's life-giving flood: water and his precious blood." It seems likely that Luther had Noah's flood in mind since Peter makes the connection between baptism and that flood in I Peter 3:20–21: "When God's patience waited in the days of Noah, during the building of the ark, in which a few, that is, eight persons, were saved through water, baptism, which corresponds to this, now saves you, not as a removal of dirt from the body but as an appeal to God for a clear conscience, through the resurrection of Jesus Christ." Noah's flood is a symbol of total devastation against which one is powerless unless saved by an act of God. The blood of Christ, shed in that event where death dies, becomes a life-giving flood through the waters of baptism.

A Communion hymn (210:3) makes a connection between death and the Red Sea:

> Where the paschal blood is poured
> Death's dread angel sheathes the sword;
> Israel's hosts triumphant go
> Through the wave that drowns the foe.

It is the paschal blood of Christ that takes away the power of death, which is depicted as a flood in the first verse of the same hymn:

> At the Lamb's high feast we sing
> Praise to our victorious king,
> Who has washed us in the tide
> Flowing from his pierced side.

Crossing the river Jordan into the promised land of Canaan is also an image used in hymnody. It is an image of passage, with water the threat of death through which one must pass. "When I tread the verge of Jordan," passage through which will be the "death of death and hell's destruction," I pray that God will "land me safe on Canaan's side" (343:3). Similar imagery is found in the fourth verse of 501: "Even death's cold wave I will not flee, since God through Jordan leadeth me."

## IMAGERY OF SLEEP
### Fear: Dusk  ◊  Comfort: Dawn

There are many hymns which use imagery linking the day to life, the night to sleep, and the dawning of a new day to heaven. The use of such imagery is particularly strong in the vespers liturgy and hymnody. Perhaps the best known of such hymns is *Abide With Me* (272). "Eventide" is the image for the ebbing of "life's little day."

> Hold thou thy cross before my closing eyes,
> Shine through the gloom, and point me to the skies;
> Heaven's morning breaks, and earth's vain shadows flee;
> In life, in death, O Lord, abide with me.

The same close connection between the end of day and the end of life is expressed in another familiar evening hymn which expresses the hope that "I may dread the grave as little as my bed" (278:3). It is the protecting presence of God which takes the fear out of going to sleep at night: "Guard us waking, guard us sleeping, and, when we die, may we in your mighty keeping all peaceful lie" (281:3). If going to sleep is like dying in the arms of Christ, then waking up is like the dawning of heaven, as suggested in the following verse:

All praise to thee, who safe hast kept
And hast refreshed me while I slept.
Grant, Lord, when I from death shall wake,
I may of endless light partake.

The same imagery of waking up in heaven is used in the chorale (325:3) which Bach used to conclude the St. John Passion:

O Lord, thy little angel send
When'er my mortal life shall end,
To bear my soul to heaven.
My body in its chamber keep;
All torment do thou distant keep,
Till thy last call be given.
And then from death awaken me,
That these poor eyes their Lord may see;
See, Son of God, thy glorious face,
My savior and my fount of grace.
Lord Jesus Christ, O hear thou me, O hear thou me,
Thee will I praise eternally.

Rest appears again and again as a positive image of life's end. Weary ones will rest and enjoy endless sabbaths (337). The saints will take their rest when they live at home with God (314:3). The end of life's journey is depicted as "the peaceful rest" (334:3). So also the saints will "from their labors rest" (174:1).

## IMAGERY OF BATTLE
### Fear: Death's Power  ◇  Comfort: Christ's Victory

Imagery of warfare between the forces of death and the forces of life is used frequently in hymnody. The imagery works well because in our experience death seems so powerful. There is no human defense against it that ultimately prevails; at best our defenses are delaying actions. Only the imagery of a power greater than death can offer hope to the vanquished.

The "kingdom of death," "the realm of death," and "the reign of death" are all images of the power of death. The imagery of this "strange and dreadful strife" was strongest in the late Middle Ages when the power of death, especially in the plague, could not be ignored. Death is frequently depicted as a triumphant king in medieval art. With a sword in hand death rides unopposed on a mighty horse or appears enthroned as a king in a triumphal victory march.

In hymnody, however, this enemy is vanquished again and again, defeated by Christ in the very moment that death appears to be the victor. That theme is particularly strong in Easter hymns like 134:2.

> It was a strange and dreadful strife when life and death contended;
> The victory remained with life, the reign of death was ended.
> Holy Scripture plainly says that death is swallowed up by death,
> Its sting is lost forever.

The same battle motif is used in hymn 135:

> The strife is o'er, the battle done;
> Now is the victor's triumph won!
> Now be the song of praise begun.
>
> The powers of death have done their worst,
> But Christ their legions have dispersed,
> Let shouts of holy joy outburst.
>
> He broke the age-bound chains of hell;
> The bars from heaven's high portals fell.
> Let hymns of praise his triumph tell.

## IMAGERY OF IMPRISONMENT
### Fear: Bondage  ◊  Comfort: Liberation

A variety of hymns refer to "the grasp of grave" (96:2), the "grip of death" (295:2), and the "embrace of death" (189:1). One of the most frightening of such images is found in 539:2, "when the dark grave engulfs its prey." One is reminded of images from medieval art where death is depicted as a monster with a gaping mouth ready to devour the souls of the damned.

What brings comfort to the Christian are the images of liberation that are associated with the resurrection of the dead. Images of "bursting forth" are regularly used in Easter hymns to describe the resurrection of

Christ. Christ "rends death's iron chain" (129:5); "He broke the age-bound chains of hell" (135:4); "He burst the bars of the tomb's dark portal" (132:5); "He lay in death's strong bands" (134:1); now the "bonds are broken" (155:3).

## IMAGERY OF DEATH AS A FRIEND

Death is so consistently depicted in images of terror and dread that it is surprising to discover images of death as a friend, as in 527:6:

> And you, most kind and gentle death,
> Waiting to hush our final breath,
> Oh, praise him! Alleluia!
> You lead to heaven the child of God
> Where Christ our Lord the way has trod.

Death is also imaged as a friend in 342, where the approaching evening, sleep, and the next morning are images of a gentle and welcome death:

> I know of a sleep in Jesus' name
> A rest from all toil and sorrow;
> Earth folds in its arms my weary frame
> And shelters it till the morrow;
> With God I am safe until that day
> When sorrow is gone forever.
>
> I know of a blessed eventide,
> And when I am faint and weary,
> At times with the journey sorely tried
> Through hours that are long and dreary,
> Then often I yearn to lay me down
> And sink into peaceful slumber.
>
> I know of a morning bright and fair
> When tidings of joy shall wake us,
> When songs from on high shall fill the air
> And God to his glory take us,
> When Jesus shall bid us rise from sleep;
> How joyous that hour of waking!

## Notes

1. Triacca 38, ed., *The Temple of the Holy Spirit,* pp. 184–87.
2. Hom. 13, 1.
3. *Catachesis Mystagogica* 2.4.
4. Mark Bangert, "The Funeral Liturgy," unpublished manuscript of address given at the 1982 Liturgical Institute at Valparaiso University, Valparaiso, Indiana.
5. Richard Rutherford, *The Death of a Christian*: The Rite of Funerals (N.Y.: Pueblo Press, 1980) p. 62.
6. Gordon Lathrop, "Assembling at Sarah's Tomb: Reflections on Death and the Liturgy," unpublished manuscript of address given at the 1982 Liturgical Institute at Valparaiso University.
7. *Lutheran Book of Worship* (Minneapolis: Augsburg Publishing House, 1978).

# Part II

# Exercises in Guided Faith Imagery

# 5. How To Use Guided Imagery for Death Education and Grief Ministry

We have seen in Part I that imagery has been a powerful medium for the church's expression of faith in dealing with death and dying. That imagery is made our own through the chanting of psalms, the singing of hymns, and the praying of prayers. The guided imagery exercises in the second half of this book provide an additional resource for making that imagery our own and in some cases to spawn entirely new images. Used within the framework of traditional educational, liturgical, and pastoral care practices, guided imagery can be a powerful tool for helping a Christian face the realities of dying and grieving.

This is a "how to" chapter in which you will find step-by-step instructions on how to use a guided imagery exercise. The exercises in guided imagery which are found in Chapters 6–10 can be used privately by individuals or by a leader directing one person or a group of persons. Though I will offer some suggestions on their individual use, my chief concern in this chapter is to provide instructions to leaders on how to use guided imagery in a group setting. I will assume that the group setting is within the context of a Christian congregation, though that is not a necessary condition.

The leader need not be a pastor or a priest, though ordained clergy are likely to have more occasions for using these exercises than anyone else. Almost anyone can serve as a guide in these exercises because no special training or experience is needed. There are certain qualities (tone of voice, soothing presence) which will enhance the guided imagery process, but those qualities are not unique to the clergy and can be cultivated through practice and self-scrutiny by most laypeople. All of the direction that you will need to become an effective leader is contained in this chapter.

### Where, When, and With Whom To Use Guided Imagery

There are a variety of group settings within a Christian congregation that would be appropriate for an exercise in guided imagery. I will mention the most obvious:

(1) **Worship Services.** This is an ideal setting for guided imagery because the liturgy is already a deeper-than-intellectual experience. Homilists who are master storytellers make extensive use of imagery to draw worshipers into the story. An exercise in guided imagery could be used as part of or in place of a sermon or homily. The Lenten season or any worship service where the Scripture readings focus on the theme of death would be a good time for using guided imagery.

(2) **Religious Retreat.** A retreat setting creates a mood which is conducive to guided imagery. Those who are attending the retreat have removed themselves from their normal place and pattern of living. There is a readiness, even a hunger for reflection on spiritual concerns. It could even be a retreat on "Understanding Death and Dying," a theme that would be ideal for a Lenten or post-Easter retreat.

(3) **Bible Study.** Bible study can be very boring if it fails to make the original setting of the text come alive or if it is not relevant to contemporary concerns. The exercises in guided imagery in Chapters 6 and 7 are based on scriptural passages and invite the participants to a deeper-than-intellectual reflection on the meaning of that particular text for their own lives. After the leader becomes more familiar with the process of guided imagery, he can construct an exercise of his own to enhance the study of the Bible.

(4) **Grief Support.** Many congregations sponsor groups for the support of those who are grieving. For the most part, such groups provide a time and place for individuals to engage in the grieving which is so essential in the process of restructuring their lives without the person who is dead. Exercises in guided imagery will not only facilitate the process of grieving, but also envision a future no longer haunted by ghosts from the past.

(5) **Youth.** One of the myths of our age of death-denial is that young people do not think about death or have occasions to grieve in the

way older people do. That's why they have often been the invisible members of the family when death occurs. From my work with college students I have discovered that young people are eager to learn more about death. They have vivid imaginations and can make ready use of guided imagery, though it needs to be adapted to their needs (e.g., anticipating the loss of parents vs. anticipating their own death).

(6) **Programs for the Elderly.** Many congregations are providing special services for the increasing percentage of their membership who are in their retirement years. Groups like "The Fifty and Over Club" are particularly responsive to the use of guided imagery. Not only will they have experienced more losses and be closer to their own death, but there is usually a greater readiness at this stage of life for exploring the inner life.

## Principles of Guided Imagery

The reader should be aware of the basic principles which inform my use of guided imagery. I list them without insisting that they are the only or even the best principles to employ. A person with a different set of principles could use or adapt the exercises which follow in different and perhaps very effective ways. I will make note of alternative principles as we proceed.

The first principle is that a deeper level of experience is needed for participants to make effective use of guided imagery. It is for that reason that the beginning portion of each exercise is designed to induce a state of relaxation and readiness for what is to follow. Ira Progoff calls this a state of "twilight imagery," a state somewhere between waking and sleeping which functions like a spawning ground for images. All methods of guided imagery assume the importance of a trancelike state for exploring the inner world of one's own experience.

A second principle in my use of guided imagery is that the spirituality which is nurtured in the exercises should be Christian. This principle is different from that of Progoff, who is concerned about spirituality, but whose exercises in twilight imagery are unstructured and without specific content. My focus on Christian spirituality is similar to that of Father Robert Perry, who has incorporated Progoff's intensive journaling method into a program of group spiritual direction within the framework of Christian community. The difference between Progoff's journaling method and Perry's program of spiritual direction is the difference between spirituality in general and a focused spirituality on Christian themes. Father Perry has used Progoff's journaling tools to facilitate reflection on the classic narratives of biblical literature. My plan is similar to that of Perry, though I narrow the focus for reflection even more by using biblical passages on the theme of death and dying.[1]

A third principle in my use of guided imagery is that structured exercises work better than unstructured ones for focusing on a particular theme like death and dying. Some people prefer unstructured exercises, where imagery emerges spontaneously from the person participating in the exercise, and they are likely to resist specific directions. However, the feedback which I have received suggests that most people would rather have specific images to reflect on as long as they are encouraged to rely on the uniqueness of their own experience and understanding of those images. The death of Christ does not have the same meaning to everyone, but the cross provides an image common to all Christendom for reflecting on the themes of death and dying. Exercises based on the cross provide ample opportunity for individuals to reflect on that theme with imagery that emerges out of their own inner world of experiencing.

One of the principles of Progoff's method which I regard as essential for the process of guided imagery is what he calls "active privacy." He defines it as follows:

> *Active privacy* is the basic means of inner contact available to an individual. It does not mean working alone, nor does it mean holding ourselves aloof from others, for privacy does not involve a physical place or a physical condition. Privacy is primarily an inner place and a quality of being. Especially it is the condition of being that is established in a person when his attention is focused toward nurturing the seed and deepening the roots of his life. *Active privacy* is the relation of a person to himself as he works with the inner process of his life.[2]

It is important for all participants in these exercises to know that their privacy will not be invaded. These exercises are deeply personal, but they need not be interpersonal to be effective. It will be difficult for individuals to get maximal value out of these exercises if they are not assured of complete privacy.

The fifth principle which I advocate for the use of guided imagery is that a group setting maximizes the effectiveness of guided imagery. This principle may seem to be in contradiction to the previous principle emphasizing privacy, but it has been my experience that the group environment provides an outer support for the private inner experience. Being in a group does not necessarily imply group interaction in either verbal or behavioral ways. One can draw strength from the presence of others while being engaged in an intensely personal experience. Each person in the group works individually on his own life, but the nurturing presence of the body of Christ is a vital ingredient in facilitating that work. A group worship experience operates in much the same way. The ritual behavior (listening, praying, singing, kneeling) has little group interaction, and yet for most people worship provides a rich sense of common life.

Privacy does not mean isolation, but it does mean that each person is responsible for her own spiritual journey. Individual responsibility is the sixth principle underlying my use of guided imagery. Can you be sure that everyone can assume responsibility for his own journey? Is there a danger that the process will weaken the defenses of people with egos unable to withstand the onslaught of powerful pathological forces within them? Will they not be rendered defenseless when strong emotions begin to surface? I think not. I have yet to encounter or hear about an instance where guided imagery has exacerbated someone's pathology or made it more difficult for that person to cope with life in general or with the particular life issues that were the focus of the exercise. Participants may be deeply affected by the experience, of course, and some will cry. But they will not fall apart. People can be trusted to use an intuitive wisdom in processing their own inner experience, and I have learned to trust that wisdom both as a participant and as a leader of such exercises. There is a big difference between the active privacy of guided imagery and the intrusive probing of an analytical therapist.

## Steps To Follow

Let's assume that you're intrigued enough by the process of guided imagery by this point to want to give it a try. You may find yourself hesitating because you've never done anything like this before. What follows is a step-by-step procedure for what you are to do. This is all of the direction you will need. No workshops required. No expensive training. No fancy credentials. The only requirement is that you trust the process and yourself sufficiently to give it a try. Later on in this chapter you will find some hints on improving your skills as a leader.

### Finding a Suitable Place

Almost any place can work. I once did a guided imagery exercise for nurses in a meeting room on the corridor of a busy hospital that doubled as a cloak room. Not only was there the normal noise of a typical hospital, but also a stream of nurses coming in to get their coats at a shift change. Even there the feedback was positive, but I doubt that anyone but nurses could shut out all the distractions. I must hasten to add that I've also had the opposite experience when I attempted to do a guided imagery exercise for college students who could distinctly hear a lecture from an adjoining classroom. That distraction ruined the exercise for most of the participants.

Examine the room that will be used with an eye and ear toward its use for guided imagery. Are the walls thin? Is there a radiator with a loud hiss? Is there a neon light that flickers? Is there a telephone in the room? Any way that you can control potential detractions will enhance the guided imagery exercise for those who are participating.

Ideally, the room used for guided imagery should have good ventilation, mild to cool temperature, comfortable chairs, and a location where outside interruptions can be controlled, if not eliminated. There is an advantage to dimming the lights, if that is possible.

The experience will be enhanced if the room contains some common Christian symbols (e.g., a cross, a burning candle, an open Bible) to help focus attention and increase spiritual awareness. Such symbols beckon that to which they point and at the same time invite the person who is meditating to a deeper level of consciousness. The symbols should be familiar to those who are participating in the experience, having the power to evoke a sense of mystery and meaning.

### Preparing the Participants

The use of guided imagery in a sermon precludes all but the most minimal preparation, but there are already assurances in that setting that the leader can be trusted and that privacy will not be invaded. Whenever possible, however, the leader should explain the process of guided imagery to the participants.

The purpose of inducing relaxation should be explained, as well as the use of music in the background. Participants should be assured that they will at all times remain in complete control of the experience, that the leader cannot lead them to experience anything that they do not wish to experience, and that they can withdraw from the experience anytime they wish by simply ignoring the directions being given. Having given them these assurances, the leader should encourage participants to enter as fully as they can into the experience because the value of the exercise will be in direct proportion to their ability to surrender themselves to the process.

Comment on the importance of silence and the difficulty most Americans have with periods of silence. Urge all participants who have watches which beep on the hour to put them in their pockets or pocketbooks.

Most of the exercises include a writing portion. If writing is to be part of the exercise, tell the participants in advance and explain the purpose that it serves. Make sure that every person is equipped with paper and pen. It's all the equipment that they will need.

Assure the participants that they will not be asked to share what they experienced or wrote with anyone else in the room, including the leader. You may on occasion wish to encourage those who so choose to share their experience at the end of the exercise. If so, supply that information at the beginning of the exercise. Since trust is so crucial to the process, no surprises should be allowed to undermine it.

Each exercise has a set of specific directions for the leader at the beginning of the exercise. Be sure to read them carefully even though you may choose to ignore some of the directives.

## *Inducing a State of Relaxation and Readiness for Guided Imagery*

Guided imagery calls for a level of awareness deeper than the ordinary, everyday consciousness of the waking day. A meditative atmosphere is needed for people to enter what Progoff calls the realm of "twilight imagery" or what Watkins calls a "waking dream." A state of relaxation somewhere between waking and sleeping is needed before a person can enter the realm of twilight imagery.

The physical environment will either enhance or impede the state of relaxation. Comfortable chairs should be provided whenever possible. If the room is large enough and the floor is carpeted, you may want to suggest the option of lying down. This will enhance the relaxation (sometimes too much), but it creates a problem if writing is part of the exercise. Lights that can be dimmed will also facilitate the relaxation.

It is much easier to reach a state of relaxation appropriate for imagery if you are listening to the soothing voice of someone speaking to you, even if that voice is your own coming from a tape recorder. The same is true for the guided imagery portion. It is extremely difficult to be your own guide. It would be like asking your left brain to guide your right brain, forcing you into a constant changing of gears. This is the strongest single argument I know for having a leader for these exercises. For the same reason the reader should not judge the value of these exercises by a casual reading of them. Reserve judgment until you've tried the experience yourself.

At the very beginning of the relaxation portion of the exercise, immediately after explaining the process, I start a tape recording of soft background music to help facilitate relaxation. Not any music will do. Music with words, a strong melody, or a pronounced beat will draw attention to itself and away from inner reflection, and some people will be distracted no matter what music you choose. I would recommend the music of Steven Halpern, such as *Comfort Zone,* or Pachelbel's *Canon in D*.

As participants relax, encourage them to close their eyes in order to focus awareness on what is happening in the inner world of their experience. Most of the waking day our eyes are focused on what is going on outside us, and we rarely turn our attention inward to explore what is happening in the center of our selves. There may be some resistance to this for fear of losing control or perhaps going to sleep, but it's much harder to focus and maintain our attention on what's going on inside if our eyes are wide open. Do not insist on closed eyes, however. Some people can engage in guided imagery with their eyes open. Others feel anxious when their eyes are closed. Whatever the reason, respect the person's intuitive wisdom in making the correct judgment.

Each of the exercises in guided imagery in the following chapters has an opening section designed to induce relaxation and a state of readiness for the guided imagery to follow. Many of these inductions are tailored specifically for the particular exercises where they are used, but many of the others can be easily exchanged for each other. Depending upon preference, the leader may take elements from a number of exercises to construct his own induction exercise.

You will notice a focus on breathing in many of the inductions found in the exercises. Breathing is a natural rhythm of the human body, and to invite people to attune themselves to that rhythm is a way to quiet the self and enter its internal life. Breathing rises from the roots of our being and has profound religious meaning to Christians. It was God's breath which enlivened Adam, and our breathing is a reminder that our every breath is a gift of life from God. So to be attuned to our breathing is not only to be attuned to our inner being but also to the God who is the source of our being.

The purpose and value of inducing relaxation and a state of readiness for guided imagery is stated with clarity by Progoff:

> Sitting in quietness, our eyes close. We let this take place gradually. It is as though the stillness and softness of our breathing draw our eyelids together so that they seem to close of themselves. We realize that when our eyes close gradually and softly in this undeliberate way the darkness we enter is not unpleasant. It is, in fact, rather comfortable. It carries an atmosphere of calmness with it as we let ourselves quietly drift into the twilight level. Our attention has naturally readjusted itself and has turned by its own tempo to the inward dimension. Here we may perceive the realities of life, and especially the realities of our personal life, in the varied aspects of their symbolic forms. This *inward beholding* gives us the added vantage point of a depth perspective.[4]

To describe the deepening process by which a person moves to a level of awareness where imagery is the natural mode of expression, Progoff uses the symbol of a well connected to an underground stream. Each person has her own well distinct from every other. The well is a metaphor of depth, and entering it by means of the mind's eye is helpful imagery for going down into the depths of oneself. The underground stream is Progoff's imagery for a transpersonal connection to the source of all wells. When we have gone deeply enough into our wells we "find that we have gone *through our personal life beyond our personal life.*"[5] The symbol of the underground stream is very close to Paul Tillich's symbol of the "ground of being." Both of these symbols of transcendence are metaphors of depth rather than height. Both are symbols of God without specific content. Both invite a form of meditation that takes us to the deepest levels of human experience and facilitates our most profound awareness of the presence of God.

I find this imagery helpful, though Christians will be quick to link the underground stream to the "living water" of which Jesus spoke to the woman at the well, which will become "a spring of water welling up to eternal life" (Jn 4:7–15). Jesus is the source of the water of life to whom we turn for the nourishing and replenishing of our individual lives. Moving deeply into the well of our spiritual lives is surely not the only or even the most important way of deepening our faith, but it is a valuable resource for expressing and deepening our faith.

It would be hard to overemphasize the importance of inducing the proper state of relaxation. You can facilitate it by choosing the right location, greeting participants as they come, carefully explaining the nature and purpose of guided imagery, playing soft and soothing music in the background, speaking slowly and softly as you read the induction, and pausing between phrases as you read. All those factors are important and contribute to a state of relaxation and readiness for guided imagery.

You can also do one or two physical exercises immediately before the induction to facilitate relaxation. A few examples are: rotating the neck on its axis, rotating the shoulders up and around, tensing muscles and relaxing them, giving the person next to you a shoulder rub. This is a useful thing to do if you need to make a transition from a more stressful activity to an exercise of guided imagery.

### Leading the Guided Imagery

The pacing and the tone of voice of these exercises are as important as the content of the guided imagery. Proper pacing calls for slower speech than normal and frequent pauses. I have suggested appropriate places for pauses in the induction because it is so important that this portion of the exercise be done slowly and with frequent pauses. Three dots . . . represent a short pause (about 2 seconds); five dots. . . . . represent a longer pause (about 5 seconds). Pauses are also needed in the guided imagery portion, and some suggestions are given for longer pauses (e.g., 1–2 minutes).

Don't assume that nothing is going on during periods when you pause. The pause will seem much longer to you than to those you are guiding because you don't have anything to do but keep track of the time, and time always seems to go slower when you're watching a clock. Get feedback from participants about pacing. Chances are that you'll be going too fast rather than too slow, at least initially. These are only suggestions. Each leader will need to develop his own style through the experience of leading the exercises.

Your tone of voice is also crucial for leading these exercises. A soft and gentle voice will be most effective because such a voice facilitates relaxation and soothes the spirit. Only rarely and for special effects will the voice of the leader be loud and intense. Not only is such a voice jarring, but it draws attention to the speaker rather than facilitating the inner journey of the person you are directing. Listening to yourself on a tape recorder and getting feedback from participants will help you make whatever adjustments are necessary to develop a tonal quality that will work well for guided imagery.

Though pacing and tone of voice are important, it is the content of the exercise that determines its worth. The leader should not only be familiar but comfortable with the content of these exercises. If an exercise seems too anxiety provoking to you, your discomfort with the exercise will be conveyed through your tone of voice. Experiment. Change what is jarring to you. Add what you think is missing. Eliminate what seems superfluous or distracting. In other words, make the exercise your own. After you become more familiar with the process, you should be able to construct an exercise of your own based on one of your favorite portions of Scripture or related to a particular situation.

## The Writing Portion of the Exercise

Almost all of the exercises in this volume include some form of writing. The writing portion of the exercise is at the same time the most valuable and the most problematic part of the process of guided imagery. It is possible to eliminate the writing portion of most of the exercises with only minor adaptations, but I would urge you not to do that for reasons that I will suggest in the remainder of this section.

Spontaneous expression of feeling and thinking is the kind of writing that is called for rather than exposition or interpretation. The most effective writing will not be *about* the imagery but rather an expression of it. Interpretation is another form of writing which calls for the skills of analysis and critique, useful tools for evaluation, but guaranteed to short-circuit the process of guided imagery.

Unless participants have kept a journal of some kind, they are not likely to have done much writing that could be called a spontaneous expression of feeling and thinking. As a result, you will get feedback to the effect that their deeper level of experience was lost when they were asked to write. You will need to encourage participants to let their pens simply be a medium for expressing what they are experiencing.

The writing does not have to be in the form of sentences. It might be a series or cluster of words or phrases. Nor does the writing need to be linear, the very form of which (line by line) implies a left-brain, analytical mode of thinking. Suggest the idea of putting separate words in a cluster, letting feeling and ideas flow out of that center.

It will be helpful if you regularly suggest to participants that they open their eyes only a slit while writing and then close them again. They will also find it easier to remain at a deeper level of experience if they put their pens down when they are not writing. Above all, they need to think of the writing as an expression of their experience, not a description of it and certainly not an analysis of it.

Why is the writing so important? Full and complete expression of the imagery takes place only in the writing, and writing preserves the imagery for further reflection at a later time. There is also a feedback effect that is achieved by writing down non-judgmental accounts that record the imagery and affect of our inner lives. The feedback effect comes in reading these accounts back to ourselves. This may be done in the presence of a group or in private. If done privately, the account should be read into a cassette recorder and then played back. The writing and the reading are not done for purposes of sharing with others, but to deepen the inner process within oneself. A further dimension of feedback comes through reading entries made one, two, or ten years before. It is for this reason that you should encourage participants to date each account. One's attitude toward death is likely to change from one year to the next, and certainly from one decade to the next.

The risk of expressing imagery in words is that concepts force imagery into a structure which distorts its meaning. What was necessarily ambiguous in the experience becomes one and only one thing when put into words. The rational ego's need to order reality by means of structured categories like time, space, and cause and effect can distort the non-progressing and simultaneous aspects of many images. In spite of these difficulties, writing is a constructive and rewarding part of exercises in guided imagery. Its value will prove itself as you use it regularly.

### Closing the Exercise

After allowing sufficient time for writing or reflection, the task of the leader is to gently lead the participants out of the guided imagery experience and back into the world of everyday experience. I have suggested the amount of time to be allowed for reflection and writing at the end of each of the exercises, but the leader will need to use her judgment about whether to allow more or less time than that. Under normal circumstances adults can be expected to use as much time for writing as you will allow. It is important not to bring the exercise to a close too speedily. A typical closing statement will be something like the following: "As you are ready, bring your writing to a close and gradually come back from the world of your imagination to the room where we have been conducting this exercise. Take the time to do this gradually. You will not be rushed." Having said that, allow them sufficient time to complete the process. It is easy to underestimate the time that is needed since you as the leader do not need to make the same transition from one world of experience to another. Leave the music on during this transition period. Turning off the music will break the mood and be the signal that the exercise is over.

### Getting Feedback

For the first three or four times that you use guided imagery, I would encourage you to get feedback from the participants at the end of the exercise. You will probably get the most honest and helpful feedback if you ask participants to fill out a form and keep it anonymous. For those who might find it helpful, I will list the questions which I included on the first feedback form that I used. After I received enough general information from this instrument, I devised separate forms for each exercise in order to specify elements in the exercise concerning which I needed specific feedback.

---

**GUIDED IMAGERY FEEDBACK FORM**

1. Describe in a few words (not necessarily sentences) your general reaction to the experience (e.g., couldn't get into it, went to sleep, was deeply moved, etc.).

2. What did you find distracting or disruptive (e.g., music, tone of voice, pace, rough transitions, resistance to directions)?

3. What was it that you found helpful (e.g., music, tone of voice, pace, what you were led to reflect on)?

4. What were your reactions to the writing part of the exercise? Was it helpful in clarifying and integrating the experience? Was the time allowed too much, too little, about right?

---

I devised the feedback forms to discover where the problems in the process were. What proved to be the most helpful feedback I received were the positive comments. You need to know that what you are doing is helpful to those whom you serve. Let them tell you that.

## Problems That Can Be Anticipated

Several difficulties can be anticipated as you attempt to lead people into the experience of guided imagery. For most people it will be a new experience and thus strange and perhaps weird. Keep in mind that our word "weird" is derived from the German word *werden,* meaning to become. It may indeed be a weird experience to enter the strange world of twilight imagery where the imagination is king rather than reason. Reason does not easily step aside as the primary auditor of our experience. Left-brain types are more likely to experience resistance to the process than those who give free reign to their imagination.

As you might have guessed, women generally experience much less resistance to the process of guided imagery than men. I regularly asked participants to put M (male) or F (female) on the feedback forms which they filled out. It was quite clear that women were more able to surrender the need to control their experience and were generally able to experience a much deeper level of involvement.

Restlessness of body, mind, and spirit may also be a problem for participants. Most people lead very busy lives; they're always on the move. The guided imagery exercise is likely to be a complete switch of gears for them—from busyness to inactivity, from noisiness to quiet, from outside involvement to inner reflection. That change of pace is difficult to make even if one has some training and experience in doing it, but for most participants that will not be the case. Symptoms of restlessness are thoughts that keep popping into consciousness, tension in the body, the mind wandering from what the leader is saying. Such people need longer periods for inducing relaxation and readiness for guided imagery. Restlessness can be a major impediment to guided imagery, but it need not be a roadblock.

There will be occasions for every individual when these exercises will simply not work. There can be many different reasons for this: lack of energy, physical or mental weariness, spiritual dryness, restlessness, low-grade depression, headache or some other physical malady, the content of a particular exercise, etc. Participants should be told in advance that this might happen. Since it happens to even the most celebrated mystics, they should not assume that they will respond in a similar manner all of the time. On other occasions their experience might be full of meaning.

Some participants will find themselves fighting sleep or actually dozing off. This is to be expected, especially if the exercise comes at the end of a busy day or after a heavy meal. For the exercise to succeed it is necessary to induce a state of relaxation that is close to sleeping. When possible, encourage participants to take a fifteen minute nap before attending a session where guided imagery will be used.

As indicated earlier, resistance, which may or may not be conscious, can be anticipated. It may be resistance to the process of guided imagery that is prompted by fear of losing control or suspicion of exploring one's inner thoughts and feelings. Even those who find the process of guided imagery generally useful may become resistant to some particular exercise that invites them to deal with some segment of their experience which they are not ready for. Most of the time resistance is an unconscious defense mechanism which keeps a person from becoming deeply involved in the guided imagery. As is true with all defense mechanisms, resistance should be respected. It's one of the ways in which participants maintain control of their own experience. The resistance, if it is psychological rather than ideological, will disappear when the person feels safe enough to participate without feeling threatened beyond his or her capacity to cope with it.

Finally, some participants will likely respond negatively to the specificity of directions in many of the exercises. This is likely to be the case for those who have previous experience with guided imagery and self-hypnosis. Such people prefer a more unstructured form of guided imagery because it permits them much more control over the process and allows greater flexibility for creative construction of imagery. The drawback to this approach is that it makes it easier to avoid experiences which might prove uncomfortable, and most of the exercises in this volume have some level of discomfort associated with them.

## Improving Your Skill as a Leader

In my judgment participation in exercises of guided imagery is both a necessary and a sufficient condition for serving as a leader in such exercises. It is a necessary condition because you cannot have a feel for and appreciation of guided imagery unless you have done it yourself. You need to be sold on the value of what you are doing before you try to encourage others to do it, much less lead them in the process. It is a sufficient condition because no other training or experience is needed in order to be an effective leader.

What if there is no opportunity for you to be a participant in a group led by another? There are two ways to get the needed experience. You can either purchase a cassette tape done by another leader, such as myself, or you can make one yourself. If you choose the latter option, read one of the exercises into a tape recorder as if you were guiding another person through the exercise, and then play the tape back for yourself. Of course, you must listen to the tape, your own or that of another leader, as a participant in the exercise. That means that you must find a time and a place where you will not be interrupted, and you must submit yourself to the full discipline of the exercise, including the writing portion. This can be a positive experience of self-care and ought to be done primarily for that reason rather than its utility value in preparing you to serve as a leader.

It will be valuable for you to record one of these exercises and play it back even if you have had experience as a participant in guided imagery. This time listen critically to the tone of your voice. Is it gentle or harsh? soft or hard? soothing or abrasive? Listen to the pace. Is it fast or slow? jerky or smooth? Listen to the emotional quality of your voice. Is it warm and inviting or cool and aloof? Is your voice flat or does it convey feeling?

After you practice with a tape recorder in the manner suggested above, the next step is to serve as a guide for one other person, asking for some feedback on your tone of voice and pacing. This person should first of all attempt to enter deeply into the experience. Only after it is completed should he reflect on the quality of the experience and provide you with feedback. You are now ready to use these exercises in a group. When you do, ask for feedback from the group in writing, making sure that the responses are anonymous (suggested form under *Steps*). Don't assume that you know how you sound to others. Not only will this help you to identify problem areas, but it will also improve your self-confidence as you realize how meaningful these exercises can be to people.

When you have conducted several exercises and received some feedback from the participants, you will have a clear sense of how effective you are as a leader, what you might do to improve your skills, and how you might adapt the exercises to better serve your needs. In time you will be able to construct your own exercises, not only for the ministry of death and dying, but for almost any area of pastoral ministry.

## Conclusion

Guided imagery is a powerful tool for activating the imagination in any area of faith and life, but it is particularly powerful for the imaging of faith in relation to experiences of death and dying. Many of these experiences, such as the anticipation of our own dying, can only be approached through the imagination; still others, like the anticipation of life after death, are even more remote from our everyday experience. And what is accessible to our experience may be too full of anxiety and foreboding to allow easy access to our normal ways of integrating experience into the totality of our lives.

Faith provides the spiritual undergirding that is needed to incorporate the experiences of death and dying into our daily lives. It is only with images of faith that we can encounter death without fear, and guided imagery can help us to fashion those images in a way that is true to our own unique experience of the God who gained the victory over death in Christ Jesus.

You have been given a rationale for guided imagery and the step-by-step procedure for using it. All that remains is a decision on your part to try it. If you find yourself hesitating to do so, check inside yourself for the reasons why. Is it because this is not a recognized method for doing pastoral ministry or because you've never done it before? Who says that new is bad? The issue is whether the method fits the need, not whether it's new or not. Are you afraid that you'll fall flat on your face and feel like a fool? It's natural to be self-conscious when you do something new. Can you remember the first time you preached or conducted a Bible class? Are you worried that people will regard the exercise as too morbid or get too emotionally involved? For a long time it was mistakenly assumed that people didn't want to talk about their dying or couldn't handle it. Could it be that such an assumption is holding you back?

My suggestion to you is one that you've undoubtedly heard as a child or given as a parent: try it before you decide whether you like it or not. That advice is as applicable to methods of ministry as it is to trying out a new food. I think you will be pleasantly surprised at how effective this methodology is for helping people deal with a deeply personal issue which evokes many emotions, both positive and negative.

Where is a good place to begin? You will probably form your own judgments about that as you read through these exercises. I think that the very first exercise in Chapter 6 is a good choice for your first try at guided imagery. The exercise creates an imaginary situation that invites identification without being too anxiety provoking. The first exercise in Chapter 7 would also work well as a first attempt. It is especially meaningful to adults who were baptized as infants.

Any book that you review as a practical resource for ministry should not be put on the shelf until you have decided when and where you can experiment with it and make a final judgment about its usefulness. Be sure to make that decision for yourself and those whom you serve before you put this book away.

*Notes*

1. I had the privilege of being a participant in the first experimental program of group spiritual direction conducted by Father Perry in 1982, at which

time both he and I were Fellows at the Center for Faith Development at Emory University, Atlanta, Georgia.

2. Ira Progoff, *At a Journal Workshop* (New York: Dialogue House Library, 1975), pp. 48f.

3. Steven Halpern's music can be obtained from Halpern Sounds, 1775 Old Country Road #9, Belmont, Cal. 94002.

4. *At a Journal Workshop,* p. 80.

5. Ibid, p. 47.

# 6. Guided Imagery Exercises from Within the Psalms

All of the exercises in this chapter use one of the psalms as their point of departure. The title of the chapter suggests that the exercises are from "within" the psalms rather than based on the psalms because the psalms are so much a part of the exercises. What makes the psalms such a powerful vehicle for guided imagery is that the psalmist speaks so directly out of the experience of faith, and the language he uses is so often the language of imagery. That's why the psalms are used so regularly for meditation and prayer. Guided imagery based on Scripture is a form of personal meditation, whether that be done while one is alone or in the presence of others.

In Chapter 2 we examined some of the images of faith and hope used in the psalms in relation to the experience of death and dying. Many of those images are used in the following exercises. You may find it helpful to review that section of the book before doing any of the following exercises, though that is not necessary in order to be able to use the images in these exercises.

Each exercise is preceded by a brief introduction which describes the content of the imagery and provides special instructions where those are needed. The first paragraph of the script in each exercise is designed to induce relaxation and a state of readiness for the guided imagery to follow.

## PSALMS 90 AND 121  ◇  Deliverance From a Life-Threatening Crisis

*Notes for the Leader*
The participant in this exercise will be guided through a life-threatening crisis. Though the event on which the exercise is based (mountain-climbing) is not one that the participant is likely to have experienced or

86

ever will in the future, it can be very realistic for the person who surrenders herself to the process. Psalms 90 and 121 are used to provide the framework of meaning for interpreting this experience. The leader should say something like the above to the participants, as well as telling them about the writing that they will be doing as part of the exercise. Be sure that each person is supplied with paper and pen.

Read Psalms 90 and 121 in a slow, meditative way. The three or four verses of these psalms that are included within the script are from the Revised Standard Version. Choose another translation if that seems appropriate, but make sure that the quotations in the script match the translation you use when reading the psalms before the beginning of the exercise.

After reading Psalm 90, comment on how the psalmist uses the thought of death to reflect on both the limited timespan we have and the expectation of God's wrath because of the way we use that time. After reading Psalm 121, note the emphasis on the power of God and his promise to protect us in every time of danger.

### Guided Imagery

Relax in your chair and close your eyes so that you can see what is going on inside of you rather than concentrating on what is happening outside of you . . . concentrating on the natural rhythm of your breathing . . . breathing in . . . and breathing out . . . breathing in . . . and breathing out . . . feeling the rhythm of your inner life . . . letting the rhythm of your breathing carry you easily and naturally into the realm of your interior life . . . moving more deeply into the inner recesses of your being, into the quietness of the center of your being . . . feeling the goodness of being alive at this very moment and breathing a word of praise to God for the continual gift of life which comes from him . . . preparing yourself for a spiritual journey that will take you to the very brink of death . . . letting yourself be guided along paths that your imagination can construct with ease.

In your mind's eye, picture a snow-covered mountain. Imagine yourself as part of a mountain-climbing party with a common goal to reach the top. Give yourself permission to be as young and physically able as you would need to be to engage in such a mission. You've established a base camp high up on the mountain, and five of you have been selected to make the final ascent to the peak. You feel the exhilaration and challenge of this special moment in your life.

Let yourself feel the majesty and the mystery of the mountain, its permanence and its power. As you reflect on the awesomeness of the natural surroundings, you begin to reflect on the majesty and the mystery, the permanence and the power of the God who formed mountains, the God who is from everlasting to everlasting, the God for whom a thousand years is as a passing night. Suddenly you feel quite small in relation to the majesty and mystery, the permanence and power of this mountain and the God who created it. How fragile your life seems as you carefully chip away one foothold after another into the icy mountainside until you reach a plateau. One slip and the crevasse opens its wide jaws to swallow you up. One false step and your life hangs in the balance. How solid this mountainside is in comparison to your soft flesh. How permanent it is compared to the fleeting hours and days that you have to spend on this earth. Far below you see a field of wild flowers growing on the mountainside, and you sense that your life is as fleeting and as fragile as the grass and flowers in that field—here today, gone tomorrow. So is human life in comparison to the life of a mountain, to the life of God.

Suddenly a snowstorm hits with an intensity known only high up on a mountainside, and you find yourself momentarily separated from the rest of the climbing party. Unable to see two feet in front of you, but unwilling to simply stay in the same spot, you stumble and find yourself hurtling over the steep precipice of a narrow crevasse. When you hit the bottom, you breathe a sigh of relief that you are unharmed, but then you realize you are pinned in the narrow crevasse, unable to move. You call out with all your might but hear only the howling wind in return. You hope and pray that others in the party will find you, but you know your life hangs in the balance, and that it's only a matter of time until the bitter cold claims your life. Feel the cold of that place as it gradually penetrates into a body unable to move. Hear the howling wind of the winter storm. Experience the loneliness and the isolation of being left alone to die. **(Pause for 1 minute)**

Unable to do anything but wait, you find your whole life passing before you as if it were projected on a screen. As each passing event appears on the screen, you hear a voice in the background intoning the same word again and again, "GUILTY, GUILTY, GUILTY." As scene after scene reveals both the flaws and the failures of your past life, you hear in the background the faint strains of a chorus, "We are consumed by your anger; by your wrath we are overwhelmed. You have set our iniquities before you, our secret sins in the light of your countenance." You come to the gradual realization that you are in a twilight zone at the border which separates this life and the next, that the scenes of your past life are blending into the scene of the last judgment. And you wish fervently that you could relive some of the past and extend some of your days into the future. If you could be snatched from this pit, then surely you would value every year, every month, every day, every hour. And you would number your days and use each one wisely.

In time the storm passes and you are able to see above you the mighty mountain you had set out to master, only now it seems to be the master, you the vanquished. As the cold penetrates ever more deeply, numbing both body and mind, you turn your eyes one last time to view the majesty of the mountain you had set out to climb, and just over the precipice of the crevasse you see the figure of a climber preparing to descend, and you know in an instant that you will be rescued, and a whole new life opens up before you. The figure that slowly but surely makes its way down the crevasse looks bigger than life, and these words begin to form on your lips: "I will lift up my eyes to the hills. From where does my help come? My help comes from the Lord, who made heaven and earth." As you are carefully lifted from your frozen tomb by expert climbers on each side of you and assisted by them up the steep incline to the top of the crevasse, other words of the psalmist come into your mind: "He will not let your foot be moved; he who keeps you will not slumber . . . The Lord will keep you from all evil; he will keep your life. The Lord will keep your going out and your coming in from this time forth and forevermore."

After you have been brought down to a chateau high up on the mountainside, given a warm bath and some hot broth, you are placed in a warm bed in order to restore your body temperature to its normal level. As you lie in bed, looking out a picture window at a panoramic view of the mountains, still too stimulated by all that has happened to sleep, your thoughts return to the events of the day and you begin to reflect on the meaning of it all for your life and faith. Imagine yourself alone and reflective at the end of such a day. In what way do you think you are different as a result of what happened? Have your priorities in life been changed? Is God nearer or farther away for you? Has your attitude toward death changed? As you are ready, write whatever comes to your mind as you reflect on your journey up the mountain and the implications of its nearly fatal outcome for your life and faith. Let your writing be as free and spontaneous as if you were dictating it at the close of that awesome day. **(Allow fifteen minutes for writing)**

## PSALM 139 ◇ The Comforting Assurance of the Presence of God

*Notes for the Leader*

There is nothing that gives greater reassurance to the person of faith at a time of crisis than feeling the comforting presence of God. That is why Romans 8:31–39 is a favorite scriptural passage for many people. The trust that "nothing will be able to separate us from the love of God in Christ Jesus our Lord" can sustain a child of faith through the most terrifying kind of experience. Psalm 139 gives expression to that basic trust of faith, and the following exercise based on it is an invitation to experience that trust.

Tell the participants that the purpose of the exercise is to help them experience the continual presence of God in their lives. Let them know that portions of the psalm will be read during the exercise. A paraphrase of the psalm by Leslie Brandt is used in the script to personalize the psalm and make it more readily accessible for guided imagery. Use another translation or paraphrase if that seems more appropriate.

### Guided Imagery

The noise of the day's busy activity has died away. You sit in quiet now, with your eyes closed, letting the silence of the exterior world settle in your soul . . . letting your inner spirit become still . . . letting the concerns and the problems of the day fly away . . . letting yourself simply be here . . . feeling yourself drifting gently down a slope that leads to your inner self. It is a gradual and pleasant downward movement toward the center of your self, ever deeper and deeper. It is a quiet and peaceful place to which you go, a room within yourself to which only you have access. It is a comfortable room, furnished by you as a place where you can go to be alone and to meditate. Picture yourself there right now, relaxing and reflecting on the presence of God in your life.

O God, you know me inside and out, through and through.
Everything I do,
> every thought that flits through my mind,
> every step I take,
> every plan I make,
> every word I speak,
You know, even before these things happen.
You know my past;
You know my future.
Your circumventing presence covers my every move.
Your knowledge of me sometimes comforts me, sometimes frightens me;
But always it is far beyond my comprehension.

Feel the presence of God with you in this room at this very moment. He is closer to you than you are to yourself. He knows you better than you know yourself. Feel his presence all around you—above and below, in front and behind, to your left and to your right. Feel God in your breathing in and out. Imagine in your mind's eye God breathing life into you as he did into Adam. Think of your breath as the breath of God. Feel the comfort and assurance of God's total presence being there all of the time in just the way that you are experiencing it now. What form does that presence take when you imagine it? Let your imagination have free reign in picturing God's presence as you feel it right now. Don't be fearful about making it too earthy. What comes into your mind when you say after me: God is closer to me than I am to myself. It is a mystery I cannot master, but an assurance to which I cling. **(Pause for 1–2 minutes)**

There is no way to escape you, no place to hide.
If I ascend to the heights of joy,
> you are there before me.
If I am plunged into the depths of despair,
> you are there to meet me.
I could fly to the other side of our world
> and find you there to lead the way.
I could walk into the darkest of nights,
> only to find you there to lighten its dismal hours.

Imagine yourself traveling alone on a dark and stormy night. You have car trouble and are unable to go further. You find shelter in an old abandoned house. The place is dark and dreary, but it's dry and there's a dilapidated old bed and mattress on which you can rest until morning. You fall into a restless sleep that is filled with scary dreams. Suddenly you are awakened from a nightmare by the sound of a creaky door and footsteps. You remain perfectly still, frozen by fear, expecting the worst. . . . And then you are surprised to hear the voice of a trusted friend or family member calling your name, and the fear that filled your entire being is immediately replaced by an inner peace. The darkness is suffused with light, the loneliness filled with presence, the fear replaced by peace. **(Pause for 30 seconds)**

As your body, mind, and spirit relax, you are aware that the peace you feel is a peace beyond understanding and the presence you feel is the presence of a beyond in our midst. Only a sacred presence could offer such a profound assurance that there can be no darkness that is not suffused with his light, no death that is not filled with his life, no place that is not filled with his presence, no time when he was not, is not, or will not be. Let the calmness and quietness of that reassurance fill your inner spirit so that the words of the psalmist may be your own: "I have calmed and quieted my soul, like a child quieted at its mother's breast; like a child that is quieted is my soul." **(Pause for 1–2 minutes)**

> You were present at my very conception.
> You guided the development of my unformed members within the body
>      of my mother.
> Nothing about me, from beginning to end, was hid from your eyes.
> How frightfully and fantastically wonderful it all is!

With the aid of your imagination, reenter your mother's womb and experience what that part of your existence might have been like. Feel the safety of that protected environment. Feel the goodness of being in a place that provides a perfectly controlled temperature day and night. Feel the satisfaction of being full inside, never hungry or thirsty and never too full. Feel the surge of growth within you and the realization of new powers that are developing constantly. And now feel the presence and power of God there providing the protection, controlling the environment, feeding you, and fashioning your body and mind into the wholeness of the unique and unrepeatable person that is you. From within the security and warmth of that safe place, hear the promise of

God which reaches back to the earliest beginnings of you: "You are my child, the apple of my eye. My love for you will never cease. Wherever you go, my arms will be reaching out to hold you and bless you." **(Pause 1–2 minutes)**

With the aid of your imagination move now to the very end of your life. Experience the hostility of an environment that offers neither the safety nor the nurture that you have counted on from before the time you were born. Experience the loss of the vital powers of body, mind, and spirit. Experience the loneliness of approaching the gates of death through which you must go alone to face a future that is as unknown to you as was the world into which you were born as an infant. As you move inexorably to the moment of your dying, I want you to picture yourself in the womb of God, in the safety of her inner being, nourished by the food of eternal life, about to be born into a world that is beautiful and exciting beyond your wildest dreams. Within the security of that womb, experience death as life, darkness as light, the end as a new beginning.

When you feel ready, write what you are feeling and thinking when you reflect on the comforting assurance of the presence of God in your past, in your present, and in your future. Keep your writing close to your experience, like that of the psalmist. What you feel is as important as what you think. Don't worry about grammar or complete sentences. Say what is there, letting the pen simply record the imagery and expressiveness of your inner spirit. **(Allow fifteen minutes for writing)**

## PSALM 23  ◊  Walking Through the Valley of the Shadow of Death

*Notes for the Leader*

Psalm 23 is everybody's favorite. Well, almost everybody. It's the one psalm that Christians are likely to know by heart, to request at a time of crisis, and to pray at the time of their dying. It meets the chief spiritual need we have in times of crisis, the need for the comforting presence of a God who will guard and guide us. But then many other passages offer that assurance as well. What is the particular appeal of this psalm? Above all else, it's the imagery: the shepherd, the wolf, the valley of the shadow of death, and the green pastures. That imagery is enhanced for Christians by the fact that Jesus calls himself the good shepherd. The vivid imagery of the psalm and its familiarity to almost everyone makes it an ideal passage on which to base an exercise in guided imagery.

Prepare the participants for the exercise by talking about the universal appeal of this psalm. Tell them in advance that the psalm will be read during the exercise and encourage them to join silently in saying the words as they are read. The translation is from the RSV. Substitute another translation if it is likely to be more familiar.

Be sure that all participants have paper and pen for writing. Tell them in advance that the writing portion of the exercise will be in the form of a dialogue script between each person and Jesus as they reflect on the experience they will be having in the guided imagery. Explain to them that they will not be writing about the dialogue but rather recording it as it happens: first what they say, then what Jesus says, then what they say, etc. This may seem a bit strange at first since each person must supply both sides of the conversation, but assure them that they will likely be surprised at how easily the dialogue flows.

### Guided Imagery

Let the stillness of the moment quiet your inner spirit as you close your eyes . . . Your thoughts are quiet now, matching the quiet of the room and the quiet of your inner spirit . . . Your energies are not moving outward but inward as you listen intently for sounds from your innermost being . . . What's going on in the world outside of you does not distract you now, for your attention is directed to the movements within your inner being . . . All of the senses by which you normally perceive things outwardly are available to you for your inward perception, enabling you to look deeply within yourself, listening for the voice of inner wisdom, feeling the moving of God's Spirit within you . . . As you settle into this region of your inner being, prepare yourself to meditate on the meaning of death with the help of the psalmist, ready to hear God's word with an inner, intuitive kind of understanding that springs spontaneously from the imagination of faith . . . opening yourself to the Spirit of God who works within you, helping you to form images of faith in your real and imagined experiences of dying. Join silently in speaking the words of the psalm as they are read:

> The Lord is my shepherd, I shall not want.
> He makes me lie down in green pastures. He leads me beside still waters;

He restores my soul. He leads me in paths of righteousness for his
   name's sake.
Even though I walk through the valley of the shadow of death, I fear no
   evil; for thou art with me; thy rod and thy staff, they comfort me.
Thou preparest a table before me in the presence of my enemies; thou
   anointest my head with oil, my cup overflows.
Surely goodness and mercy shall follow me all the days of my life; and I
   shall dwell in the house of the Lord forever.

In your mind's eye picture yourself as you were as a child, very
small and not yet able to take care of yourself. It is a warm and peaceful
summer day, and you are on a picnic with your family and a group of
other families in a beautiful meadow surrounded by grassy, low-lying
hills. You had been playing with a group of other children, but the day
was so tranquil that you wandered off from the others without the slight-
est sense of danger. But before long you realize that you are lost, and
you look around anxiously for some sign of the others. But there is nothing but the grassy meadow and surrounding hillsides. Seeing a narrow
valley that forms a passageway from one meadow to another, you decide
to follow that narrow passageway through the valley, hoping that you
will find your family on the other side. Imagine yourself as a little child
walking through a narrow valley with what seem like enormous hills on
both sides. . . . It is late afternoon. As the sun sets over one of the hills
that stand on each side of the valley, a wolf suddenly appears at the peak
of that hill, and the sun casts a shadow of the wolf many times its size
on the hill which stands across the valley. Experience the terror of seeing
that shadow of death fall across your path . . . Feel the anxiety of being
caught within "the narrows," which is the Old English term for anxiety.
**(Pause for 30 seconds)**
   You are frozen in terror as you wait for the shadow of death to cover
you and the wolf to swallow you up, but then you are surprised to see
the figure of a person approaching from behind you. Your surprise becomes delight as you recognize someone you know and trust, whomever
you wish that to be. He or she picks you up and holds you securely . . .
Feel yourself relax as the strong arms of this person enfold you and carry
you through the valley of the shadow of death to the other side, and then
put you gently down as everybody gathers around you and welcomes you
back. . . . Experience the inner peace of that moment and the level of

trust that you have in the one who came to find you when you were lost and carry you back to safety and shelter. **(Pause for 1–2 minutes)**

Let the scene shift and imagine yourself in the intensive care unit of a modern hospital . . . You are there as a patient who is critically ill and in danger of dying . . . You are aware of the shadow of death in this place, a shadow that deepens as your pulse becomes weaker. The doctors and nurses are attentive and busily manipulating machines that both monitor and regulate your vital life signs, but you can see anxiety in their eyes and sense that they are fighting a losing battle. It feels as if the wolf is at the door. **(Pause for 30 seconds)**

As your panic increases, imagine Jesus entering the room. He comes directly to you and looks deeply into your eyes with an expression of love and compassion on his face . . . Picture him picking you up as if you were light as a feather and carrying you out of the room, out of the hospital, and directly to a meadow which is bathed in sunlight and the warm breezes of a lovely spring day . . . Feel the goodness of being there and the gratitude that wells up in your heart as you are carried from a place of shadows to a place of light and life. **(Pause for 30 seconds)**

Imagine a conversation between you and Jesus as you reflect on this experience. Imagine what you would want to say to Jesus and what you think he would say to you. Let this conversation flow spontaneously without censoring or evaluating what you say to Jesus or what you hear in return. As you feel ready, let the dialogue be expressed in writing, recording both what you say and what Jesus says in return. **(Allow 15–20 minutes for writing)**

### PSALM 77 ◊ Chaos—Deliverance (Part I)

*Notes for the Leader*

This exercise is divided into two parts. One reason for the division is the length of the psalm. Another reason is that the first portion of the psalm is quite different from the second. The first part is a powerful expression of individual faith in a time of crisis. The experience is one of total devastation and God-forsakenness, but though overwhelmed by what is happening to him, the psalmist is able to remember who he is as a child of God and how God has worked wonders to rescue his people. It is that memory which is the source of his faith and the means by which he overcomes his doubt. The reading of the psalm comes in two different places within the script. The first portion is based on a paraphrase by Leslie Brandt, the second on a paraphrase by the author. Substitute another translation or paraphrase if that seems more appropriate.

The writing portion of this exercise is different from previous ones. Early in the exercise participants will be asked to make note of several crisis situations in their lives. Having selected one of those situations for further reflection, they will be asked to write about that experience at two different times. Each time they will be writing from 5–10 minutes. They will use that time more profitably if they know it is coming and approximately how long it will be. Encourage them to remain within the experiential mode of the guided imagery throughout the exercise, including the writing.

### *Guided Imagery*

As you feel ready, let your eyes close and your body relax. As your eyes close, your body becomes your home, a place where you can relax, free from outside observation and expectation. It is as if you have come home after a busy day in the outside world and now are relaxing in your favorite chair at home. You at home in your body . . . letting your breathing come quietly . . . stilling the noises within you that are echoes from the busyness of your life . . . putting the unresolved problems of the day aside . . . giving yourself permission to be here—not just with your body, but also with your mind and spirit . . . feeling your spirit quiet within you as you prepare to hear the psalmist speak from the depths of his inner experience to the depths of your inner experience . . . listening quietly to the psalmist's description of his crisis of faith as chaos threatened to overwhelm him and letting it remind you of similar crises of faith in your experience.

I cry to God in my desperation.
Out of the dark corner of my stifling loneliness I grope in vain for some
    solace or comfort.
I try to think about God, to contemplate his many promises; but my heart
    is empty, my soul as dry as dust.
I spend sleepless nights searching, waiting for God to speak to my need,
    to give me strength in my conflict.
I remember how he has responded to my prayers in times past.

But I get nothing from him now, nothing save the echoes of my own
    agonies as they are screamed into empty heavens.
I am reminded of his deeds and wonders of years past.
He demonstrated his love in his concern for his people.
His majesty and power is reflected in the great forces of nature about me.
Then why doesn't he hear my pitiful pleadings?
Why doesn't he fulfill his promises on my behalf?
Good Lord, where are you?

Imagine yourself in a situation like that of the psalmist. You have
a great need for God and his help, and you cry out to get his attention.
Your outstretched arms are like those of a drowning man reaching out
for anything to hold on to. Yet in spite of the intensity of your meditation
deep into the night, you experience only the absence of God. Is it possible that God has changed, changed from being loving and gracious to
being angry? Confusion and desperation reigns.

Let your mind drift back over the years to times when you felt like
the psalmist—alone, in great need of help, but seeing no way out. There
will likely be a number of such experiences that come to your mind. They
may or may not be related to death, but they are surely deathlike experiences in that you are facing something so overwhelming that you feel
helpless and hopeless. Jot down a word or phrase on paper that identifies
each of the experiences you recall. Open your eyes just long enough to
make the notation and then close them again so that you can retain your
concentration on inner experience. **(Pause for 2–3 minutes)**

When you have completed your list, select one of those experiences
for further reflection. . . . Choose the one that is most vivid, the one
where you felt the most helpless. In your mind's eye, reenter that experience and feel what it was like for you at that time. Where were you
when this occurred? How old were you at the time? What made this experience seem so terrible? What was the cause of the problem that you
were facing? Why did you feel so helpless to do anything to make it
better? Let yourself feel the full terror and sense of desperation in that
experience. When you have a sense that you've been in touch with the
full intensity of that experience, let your pen express on paper what that
experience was like. Words or phrases placed in a cluster may work better than sentences. Your writing may be more spontaneous if you write
in the first person: "What I'm feeling is. . . . " **(Allow 5–10 minutes
for writing)**

Putting your pen down, close your eyes and reenter the inner quietness of your centered self . . . feeling the calm and safety of this inner sanctuary . . . listening to how the psalmist moves from the pit of despair by drawing on the resources of his faith, turning from his inner desolation to the God of hope.

I will remember the mighty works of God.
I will reflect deeply on your work and meditate on the wonder of what you have done.
Your ways, O God, are unique; I could not conceive of a God greater than you!
You work wonders everywhere, but your power is especially evident among us.
You have rescued your people, the sons of Jacob and Joseph, with your strong right arm.

In the quiet of your own inner world, reenter the experience of chaos and helplessness that you were remembering before. Where is God in that experience? Does he seem distant and maybe even angry, as was the case with the psalmist? Without shutting out the feelings of chaos and helplessness, remember the God who gave you life in your mother's womb and called you to be his child in baptism. Hear him say, "You are my child, my good child whom I love very much." Feel the presence of God stilling the storm within you . . . bringing order out of chaos . . . working wonders with his power and love . . . holding you safely within the palm of his hand. Let your pen express what you feel as you turn to God in the midst of an experience of outer chaos and inner helplessness. Don't try to make it come out right. The reality of God's presence is needed, not proper piety or happy endings. If anger and resentment are there, express it. If trust and hope are there, give them a voice. If both anger and trust are there, give expression to both in whatever manner seems appropriate. (**Allow 5–10 minutes for writing**)

## PSALM 77 ◇ Chaos—Deliverance (Part II)

*Notes for the Leader*
The second part of Psalm 77 is a reflection on the exodus of Israel from Egypt through the Red Sea. Water, a symbol of chaos in much of the Old Testament, becomes a symbol of deliverance as the psalmist uses

rich imagery to vividly recall the event which stands at the center of history for Israel. The following exercise builds on this imagery by linking it to the waters of baptism, the central event in the life of a Christian. The paraphrase of the psalm in the script is by the author. Use another translation or paraphrase if that seems more appropriate. The induction is the same as for Part I. The exercise has a writing portion which could easily be discarded for use within a homily.

### Guided Imagery

As you feel ready, let your eyes close and your body relax. As your eyes close, your body becomes your home, a place where you can relax, free from outside observation and expectation . . . It is as if you have come home after a busy day in the outside world and now are relaxing in your favorite chair at home . . . You are at home in your body . . . letting your breathing come quietly . . . stilling the noises within you that are echoes from the busyness of your life . . . putting the unresolved problems of the day aside . . . giving yourself permission to be here— not just with your body, but also with your mind and spirit . . . feeling your spirit quiet within you as you prepare to hear the psalmist speak from the world of his experience to the world of your experience . . . listening quietly to the psalmist as he remembers the exodus from Egypt with all the vividness and imagination of one who seemed to be present himself when the watery chaos of the Red Sea was changed by the powerful hand of God into a safe path of deliverance to the other side.

When the waters saw you, O God, when the waters saw you, they were
   afraid; yes, the sea trembled.
Water poured out of the clouds, and thunder boomed down from the sky;
   lightning flashed like arrows from your quiver.
The crash of the thunder was in the whirlwind of your presence; the
   whole earth trembled.
Your way was through the sea, your path through the great waters; but
   your footprints were unseen.
With Moses and Aaron in the front, you led your people like a shepherd
   leads his flock.

In your mind's eye picture yourself with the hosts of Israel facing the Red Sea. There is a raging storm with lightning and thunder. Rain pours from the sky, and waves leap high on the storm-tossed sea. Behind you is the ominous sight of the Egyptian army closing off any escape route. Chaos on every side and a feeling of total helplessness within. If God is present, then it must be a God of anger and judgment. Suddenly up ahead the Red Sea parts, and a path of dry land stretches out to the other side. . . . Experience the feeling of relief at the sight of a way forward. In your mind's eye take that path through the Red Sea with walls of water on either side. As you walk, join in Israel's song of salvation: "The Lord is my strength and my song, and he has become my salvation; this is my God, and I will praise him, my father's God, and I will exalt him." **(Pause for 30 seconds)**

Let an image of watery chaos like that of the Red Sea form in your mind. Any image will do: a hurricane, a tidal wave, a storm-tossed sea. Now imagine yourself in the midst of that watery chaos, aware of the overwhelming power of destruction in untamed waters. How terrifying water can be when subject to the powerful forces of nature . . . water that threatens . . . water of death rather than water of life. **(Pause for 30 seconds)**

As you let the waves of that watery chaos wash over you, let another image of water form in your mind, the water of your baptism, the water which was the medium of the promise of God given to you at that time. Picture yourself in the church where you were baptized even though you were probably too small to remember it. Imagine being held, not only with the arms of your parent or sponsor if you were baptized as an infant, but also with the enfolding arms of God. As you feel this water of life being poured over your head or fully surrounding you as you are immersed in it, hear the voice of God speaking directly to you and only to you: "You are my good child, and through these waters I bring you safely from death to life. I promise to be with you always. Nothing will separate you from my love." **(Pause for 30 seconds)** Feel the security of being safely in the arms of the God who brought Israel safely through the Red Sea, who stilled the tempest on the Sea of Galilee, who formed you within the watery womb of your mother, and who promises you eternal life in the water of your baptism. Let the images of watery chaos and baptismal waters come together in your mind side by side. As you are ready, express in writing what you are feeling and thinking in the inner world of your experience. Let your pen express whatever is there without feeling as though it all has to fit together. Allow the various images of water that have formed in your mind to relate to each other in whatever way seems appropriate to how you are experiencing them. **(Allow 10–15 minutes for writing)**

## PSALM 4:8 AND PSALM 17:15 ◊ The Peaceful Sleep of Death

*Notes for the Leader*

Sleep is a common metaphor for death in Scripture. It should not be used with young children or anyone else for whom sleep can mean only one thing—closing your eyes and drifting into a state of unconsciousness, except for dreaming, until you wake up. For those who can think metaphorically, the imagery of sleep conveys a sense of relaxation, letting go, restfulness, security, and refreshment.

Inform the participants that the exercise is based on Psalm 4:8 and 17:15, both verses to be read during the exercise. You may also wish to read those two verses before the exercise begins. The paraphrase of the two verses in the script is by the author.

The participants should be given some idea in advance about the progression of imagery in the exercise without going into details. You might say, "We will be developing images of being comforted in a time of troubled sleep as a way of assisting you to use the metaphor of sleep as a way to imagine your dying." Some latitude is given in the selection of the person who will provide comfort in the exercise. It will be helpful for participants to know this in advance so that they can give themselves full permission to choose whomever they wish when the time comes. Be sure that all participants are supplied with pen and paper for the writing portion at the close of the exercise.

### Guided Imagery

Uncross your legs and make yourself as comfortable as you can in the chair on which you are sitting. As you close your eyes, feel the tensions of the day slowly drain away . . . Beginning at the top of your head, imagine all of the tension in your body being released and flowing away like water flowing down the side of a hill. Feel the tension drain away, beginning at the top of your head and then all the way down your body to the tips of your toes, leaving you more and more relaxed . . . feeling as you often feel before you go to sleep, very relaxed and breath-

ing more deeply . . . concentrating on your breathing and its natural
rhythm . . . breathing in . . . and breathing out . . . listening from
within a state of natural restfulness listen to words of the psalmist:

> I can lie down and sleep in peace. Because of you, I am eternally secure.
> I can look at your face with a feeling of rightness. I will be blessed with
> a vision of you when I awake.

Let images of peaceful sleep enter your mind. Remember times
when you were particularly aware of the goodness of restful sleep . . .
Perhaps it's a memory that you have of yourself as a young child going
to sleep with a parent close by. Or it may be a memory of going to bed
after solving a problem or completing a task that kept you in a state of
agitated wakefulness for a long time. Be aware of the contrast between
a state of agitated wakefulness and peaceful sleep and feel the goodness
of the gift of sleep. **(Pause for 1 minute)**
     In your mind's eye picture yourself as you were when you were a
small child about four or five years of age. If you can, picture the bed-
room and the bed on which you slept at that time . . . It is summertime
and the windows are open as you sleep peacefully in that bed . . . During
the night a thunderstorm erupts with sudden violence. Bright flashes of
lightning are followed by the deafening roar of huge thunderclaps. High
winds bend trees to the ground and snap branches as if they were match-
sticks. A feeling of terror grips your heart as you are awakened and you
frantically call for someone to come . . . Imagine the relief that you feel
as someone you love and trust enters the room, sits on the bed beside
you, holds your tense body close, and speaks reassuring words like ''It's
O.K. Everything will be all right.'' Imagine yourself lying back down
in bed, feeling safe as your hair is stroked or your back rubbed as you
gradually fall asleep . . . Imagine yourself waking up the next morning,
refreshed and revitalized. The first thing you see is the bright and shining
face of the person who had come to you during the night, almost as if he
or she had never left your bedside. Recalling the terror and the calm
which followed, reflect for a moment on the experience and the feelings
that accompany it. **(Pause for 1–2 minutes)**
     Let the scene shift to a different room and a different bed, this time
the bed on which you were lying during a time in your life when you
were physically ill, mentally depressed, or spiritually dispirited. **(Pause**

**for 30 seconds)** Picture yourself as the person you were then, experiencing once again what it was like to feel that bad. Imagine yourself falling in and out of a troubled sleep, dozing fitfully, awakened again and again by physical pain or mental anguish. As these painful and distressing feelings flood your mind and heart, robbing you of the sleep you so desperately need, imagine a loving and trusted friend entering the room and comforting you. Let the image of that scene form in your mind, and then let the scene unfold naturally, allowing that loving and trusted friend to offer you comfort in whatever way that seems appropriate to you. Feel the pain and the anguish gradually subside as you experience the soothing presence of this loving and trusted friend. Imagine yourself becoming more and more relaxed until you fall into a deep and untroubled sleep. **(Pause for 1–2 minutes)**

Once more let the scene shift to a different room and a different bed, this time the bed on which you will lie when it is time for you to die . . . Picture the room and the bed in your mind's eye. It can be wherever you wish it to be. . . . Furnish the room in any way that you wish. Make it a room in which you would like to be at the time of your dying, a room that would provide the kind of environment that you think you would need for your last days on this earth. . . . Imagine what it would be like to be close to the time of your death . . . Imagine what it would be like to go to sleep if you weren't sure that you would ever wake up again . . . Picture yourself looking into a mirror. What is it that you see? How would you describe the way that you look and feel physically . . . emotionally . . . spiritually? Do you sense that you are ready to die or do you find yourself fighting strongly against it? . . . What is the hardest thing for you about facing the end of your life? . . . Let the thoughts and feelings that come with this experience surface in your mind without any attempt at censorship or interpretation on your part. Let yourself be what you are feeling and thinking in these last hours of your life. **(Pause for 1–2 minutes)**

Now imagine Jesus entering that room and sitting on the side of your bed. If that's hard to imagine, then picture one of his emissaries, a priest or a pastor. Share with Jesus or his emissary some of what you have just written and imagine him listening intently as you do . . . After you have finished sharing what is in your heart, imagine Jesus holding you as a parent would hold a small child, soothing your troubled spirit and reassuring you that you are safe and that he will not leave you . . .

With Jesus still holding you, slowly let go of your hold on life. Feel yourself sinking more and more deeply into his arms as your breathing comes more slowly and as life ebbs away. Feel the security of falling asleep in Jesus' arms, knowing that nothing can separate you from his sheltering embrace. Hear him say in a soft, gentle voice: "I am with you always, to the close of the age" (Mt 28:20). **(Pause for 1–2 minutes)**

When you are ready, express what you are feeling and thinking in writing. Be sure to express what is there, not what you think ought to be there. Stay with the images that come and note the feelings that accompany the image. Let the images of childhood fear, adult illness, and the time of your dying flow together as you give expression to what it means to fall asleep as a beloved child of God. **(Allow 15–20 minutes for writing)**

# 7. Guided Imagery Exercises from Within the New Testament

Kierkegaard spoke of the need to become contemporaries of Christ in order for the Gospel to be personal and relevant. Rather than hearing a message about Jesus, we need to find our way into the story in order to make it our own. It is when the story of Jesus becomes part of the story of our lives that we discover its deepest meaning. Theology in both the Old and the New Testament is primarily story theology. Guided imagery is a useful tool for narrative construction, for telling the story of Jesus in such a way that we can be participants in that story, or telling our own stories in a way that Jesus can be a participant in them. That is the overall purpose in the guided imagery exercises of this chapter.

The story of Jesus, especially the story of his death and resurrection, is the story of the defeat of death. That's the story we need to get in on, the story that we need to make our own. The language of the New Testament, however, is different from the psalms. There we found language rich in imagery with many passages lending themselves readily for use in guided imagery. There is no comparable literature in the New Testament. The Gospels are narratives, and the letters of St. Paul and others are primarily problem-solving literature. The passages from the New Testament that will be used as the basis for the guided imagery exercises in this chapter will provide a point of departure for the use of imagery rather than being a direct source for the imagery. The translation used is the Revised Standard Version.

## ROMANS 6:3–5 ◇ Dying and Rising with Christ

*Notes for the Leader*

Baptism is closely linked to death in the New Testament. Jesus understood his own baptism as a baptism into death (Mk 10:38), and St. Paul in this passage considers our baptism to be a baptism into the death of Jesus. At the death of a Christian a baptismal pall is placed over the casket as a sign of eternal life.

This makes baptism the most important single event in the life of a Christian. It's an event that few Christians remember because they were baptized as infants. This exercise assumes that the participants have been baptized, and it is designed especially for those who were baptized as infants, though the script is written to include those who were older when they were baptized. Through this exercise the participants will be able to experience their baptism even though they cannot remember it. That will sound strange to them, and so they will need some advance explanation and even persuasion in order for the exercise to be meaningful. For those of you who might find it helpful, I will include in these notes an example of what you might say:

I am going to ask you with the aid of your imagination to remember the time of your baptism and to relate that reality, which is a continuous event in the life of a Christian, to the dying and rising of Christ. This will call for a creative use of your imagination since you are not likely to be able to remember the time of your baptism. All of our remembering is imaginative in that we rely on images to recall events, and what we remember is always selective and, to a greater or lesser extent, creative. Assessing an event which we cannot remember but which is important to our identity is an act of the imagination which can strengthen our identity by making the story of our lives more real.

Your baptism was a touchstone event in your life in that it marked your initiation into the family of God. Your identity as a child of God has its roots in your baptism. The story of your life would be very different without it. Yet the significance of that event rarely surfaces in the stream of everyday consciousness. How many people have ever asked you if you were baptized or what your baptism means to you? Have you ever asked others whether they were baptized and what their baptism means to them? It is highly unlikely that anyone is going to ask for the date of your baptism on a job application. Not even students entering the seminary are likely to include it in their autobiographical statements. At one time baptism was linked to the giving of a name, one's Christian name, and some parents would limit their choice of names to those found in Scripture. That is increasingly rare. The purpose of the following exercise is to establish a closer experiential link between baptism and identity, particularly in relation to the anticipation of death.

This will be a very powerful experience for many people. One man in his forties, born in Germany but a resident of this country since he was six years old, told me that he heard the trinitarian blessing in the German language. Another woman wrote this note to me:

> I would like to share with you my experience the Sunday we discussed baptism. When you asked us to meditate and turn back to our own baptism, I experienced something very special. I have always been afraid to put my head under water; in fact, I don't even like to stand under the shower and have the water splash over my face. But when you asked us to think of the waters of our baptism, I felt I was completely submerged under flowing waters and I was not afraid but felt a sense of complete trust and peace! A peace I have never felt before.

The writing portion of the exercise will be in the form of a dialogue with Jesus. Tell the participants about that in advance so it will not come as a surprise. Encourage them to write in conversational form, letting Jesus speak the words which will come naturally to them. The reason for writing the script of the dialogue rather than writing about it is to encourage the participants to stay within the experience of the imagery as they write.

The value of this particular exercise would be enhanced if it were either preceded or followed by a discussion of baptism. The purpose of the discussion would be the implications of baptism for one's personal life. A discussion of baptism in conjunction with this exercise of guided imagery would work well for confirmation class or an adult study group. If a discussion follows the use of guided imagery, make sure that no one is pressured to share what he or she experienced or wrote during the exercise.

### Guided Imagery

Sitting quietly and calmly . . . letting your breathing come slowly and regularly . . . letting your inner self become still, as still as a lake that mirrors the surrounding countryside . . . letting your tensions and worries flow from you as rainwater flows from the roof of a house . . . finding deep within yourself a center that is a place of quiet and tranquility . . . wondering at the peace you can experience in the midst of all the activity and chaos of your life . . . letting thoughts become less turbulent and feelings less intense . . . As you enter more and more deeply into your inner life, the stream of consciousness slows, flowing like a lazy, meandering stream in the middle of a broad and flat meadow. You are quiet now, as you rest quietly at the center of your self—ready to see what is hidden, to hear what is beyond hearing, to know in ways that can only be known with the inner wisdom of the soul.

Do you not know that all of us who have been baptized into Christ Jesus were baptized into his death? We were buried therefore with him by baptism into death, so that as Christ was raised from the dead by the glory of the Father, we too might walk in newness of life. For if we have been united with him in a death like his, we shall certainly be united with him in a resurrection like his.

Either by means of memory or with the aid of your imagination (or both), I want you in your mind's eye to go back to the day of your baptism. Let an image of a church setting form in your mind, either the church where you were actually baptized or one that you create in your imagination right now. Picture in your mind the worship setting in which your baptism takes place, perhaps a church service or maybe just a large family gathering. If you were baptized as an infant, imagine yourself being held securely in the arms of your mother, your father, or a godparent, or anyone that you would want to hold you. Feel how good it is to be held securely by someone who holds you well, someone you trust. Think of the people you would like to be there, people you know now as well as people who would have known you then. You can decide who should be there. Select people who have nurtured and sustained you in your identity as a child of God. Imagine them all surrounding the font or place of baptism as part of a large family gathering. **(Pause for 30 seconds)**

Imagine in your mind's eye the pastor or priest that you would like to baptize you. It can be the person who actually did baptize you or it can be a pastor or priest of your own choosing, someone you know now or someone in the past who is a wisdom figure for you. Feel the touch on your forehead as the sign of the cross is made, reminding you that you have been redeemed by Christ. Feel the water being poured over your head or imagine what it might be like to be fully immersed in water. Hear the words that are spoken as the water flows over your body: ''I baptize you in the name of the Father, and the Son, and the Holy Spirit.'' **(Pause for 30 seconds)**

Feel the cleansing which comes with the washing of the water and the promise of forgiveness. Hear the word of promise which assures you that there is nothing that you could possibly do that would make Jesus want to leave you all alone. Sense the presence of Christ all around you. Let his being flow into you and your being into him until you can say, ''It is no longer I who live but Christ who lives in me.''

As the spirit of Christ flows into you, let an image of his suffering and death form in your mind. With Christ in you and you in Christ, imagine yourself as one with him in his dying on the cross. Let the pain and suffering of his dying burn away all of the greed, all of the resentment, all of the hate, all of the pride, all of the apathy which has grown like a cancer within you. Let go of all those things, letting yourself die with Christ, surrendering your need to be in control, feeling the safety of dying when Christ is in you and you are in Christ. **(Pause for 1–2 minutes)**

Having experienced yourself as dying with Christ, imagine yourself rising with him, experiencing the wonder of passing from death to life, from sinner to saint, from damned to saved, from stranger to friend. Feel the energy of the new life that is God's gift to you. Feel its power, its permanence, its impermeability. Let images of your oneness with the risen Christ form in your mind. . . . Let them be images which transport you beyond the grasp of the jaws of death, beyond the terrors that fill your waking days and haunt your dreams, beyond the sin-sick existence that makes your soul heavy and weary. Feel the safety, the security, and the reassurance that comes with the experience of being baptized. Imagine yourself being held securely by the everlasting arms of God as you listen to a voice speaking in the same soothing tone that a mother would use with her child: ''You are baptized. You are baptized. Nothing can separate you from my love which is in Christ and embedded deeply within you. You are baptized. You are my perfect child. I will always be with you.'' **(Pause for 1–2 minutes)**

Imagine the loveliest and most delightful place that you can think of and go there with the aid of your imagination. Perhaps it's beside a waterfall on a cool summer day. Perhaps it's in the shadow of a majestic snow-capped mountain. Perhaps it's on the warm sands of an ocean shore. You are there alone. With the aid of your imagination, drink in

the richness of your surroundings with your eyes and ears and touch and smell. Enjoy the goodness of being there. **(Pause for 30 seconds)**
    In the distance picture a man walking toward you. As he draws nearer, you realize that it is Jesus. Imagine what he would look like. Look closely at his face as he approaches, especially his eyes as they make contact with yours. Rise and greet him as he comes close to where you are. Invite him to sit with you for a while and talk with him for a few moments about the meaning of your baptism. Tell Jesus what it means for you to be baptized and then listen to what you hear in return from him. Let a dialogue spontaneously unfold in your mind for a few moments. Then let your pen simply record the conversation on paper, both what you say to Jesus and what he says to you. **(Allow 15–20 minutes for writing)**

## MATTHEW 8:23–27 ◊ Finding Peace in the Center of a Storm

*Notes for the Leader*
    The reassuring presence of Christ is a trustable promise for Christians in times of storm and stress. That is why the stories of Jesus stilling the tempest and coming to the disciples during a storm are so treasured by Christians. These stories are the basis for a guided imagery exercise on the experience of Jesus' presence in our lives, and especially during stressful times.
    This exercise could be introduced by either reading or telling the story of Jesus stilling the tempest. Telling the story might well be linked to the account of Jesus coming to the disciples on a stormy night and Peter's request to come to Jesus on the water (Mt 14:22–33).

*Guided Imagery*

    As the quietness deepens within, let your eyes close and your breathing come more slowly. Imagine yourself lying on a white, sandy beach which is uninhabited by anyone else. It is a warm, sunny day with a gentle breeze pushing a few white, billowy clouds across the blue sky. Feel the warmth of the sun as you lie peacefully on the sand. Hear the soft sounds of the waves as they gently lap the shore. Let your body sink deeply into the sand and enjoy the relaxation that comes when you can put all care aside, letting your breathing come slowly and evenly, letting your spirit become one with all that surrounds you.

As you lie quietly on the sandy shore by the sea, meditating on the goodness of creation and the wonder of being alive in a world filled with such beauty, let your mind and heart be filled with an awareness of the presence of Jesus. Perhaps an image of Jesus will form in your mind. Perhaps you will remember a familiar saying of his. Perhaps you will feel his spirit within you. Whatever form it takes, be aware of his presence and what that means to you. As you lie peacefully on that warm, sandy shore, let all of your senses be open to the peace and the power of his presence. Hear his voice. Feel his healing touch. See the warmth and compassion in his face and eyes. Meditate for a moment on the meaning of his presence in your life right now. Why is Jesus important to you? What would you lose if his presence was taken away? **(Pause for 1–2 minutes)**

Imagine that there is a sailboat tied to a dock about a hundred yards down the beach. It is a seaworthy craft, large enough to have a cabin and yet small enough that it can be piloted by one person. You are an experienced sailor, and you decide to take the boat out for a sail. The winds have become stronger, and the sailing is exhilarating. Feel the movement of the boat as it knifes through the water with the wind filling the sail and the boat responsive to your skillful handling of sail and rudder . . . You become so absorbed in the thrill of the moment that you fail to notice both the receding shoreline and the gathering stormclouds on the horizon. Your heart leaps at the sound of thunder, and your nerves become taut as you turn the boat back toward shore. Suddenly the storm is upon you with raging winds, torrents of rain, and rising waves. Having secured the sail against the mast, you are at the mercy of a sea which shows no sign of mercy. As the wind rises, so do the waves—until they tower over the small craft and toss it around as if it were a matchstick. Experience the terror of being alone and helpless in a storm that threatens to end your life at any moment. As the storm intensifies and the terror in your heart increases, the words of the psalmist seem frighteningly real: "The terrors of death have fallen upon me. Fear and trembling come upon me, and horror overwhelms me. And I say, 'O that I had wings like a dove! I would fly away and be at rest' " (Ps 55:4–6). **(Pause for 30 seconds)**

As you imagine yourself in a boat on a raging sea, fearing for your life, let the image of Jesus' presence come to you in any form that seems natural to you. Perhaps you'll be aware of him sleeping in the cabin of the boat. Perhaps you'll see him coming to you across the waters of the storm-tossed sea. Perhaps you'll be aware of his spirit filling not only you but everything around you. Whatever form it takes, be aware of his presence and the difference that presence makes to you in this moment. Let that presence become as real as you can make it in your imagination, using all the powers of your perception to focus on that presence. Take a moment to meditate on the power of his presence and the difference that makes to you as you imagine yourself alone on a storm-tossed sea. **(Pause for 2–3 minutes)**

Now in your mind's eye picture a perfectly calm sea on which the sailboat peacefully rests. The storm is over, both the storm on the sea and the storm within yourself. All is quiet, and you know that your safety is assured. Once again let an image of Jesus' presence form in your mind. This time imagine yourself in conversation with Jesus. What is it that you would like to say to Jesus about what happened? What is it that you have learned about yourself? about your relationship to yourself? about your faith? about the meaning of life? about the meaning of death? Let your reflection take the form of a dialogue—you speaking to Jesus and then listening to what he would say to you. As that dialogue begins to form in your mind, write it down on paper as you imagine hearing it in your mind, both what you say and what Jesus would say to you. **(Allow 15–20 minutes for writing)**

## MARK 8:35–36  ◇  Letting Go

### Notes for the Leader

Why is it so hard for people to let go? I think it's because we act as if we own things that are really no more than gifts from God. When we experience loss, it's as if something has been forcibly taken from us against our will. A loss means loss of control. This exercise is designed to help participants consciously and willingly give up control by letting go of things which are important to them. The goal of the exercise should be discussed with participants in advance of the exercise in order to lessen their resistance to it.

If my experience with this exercise is typical, you can expect considerable resistance to the experience of letting go. The following comment on a feedback form is representative of similar comments: "The exercise worked for me, but I didn't like it. It wasn't relaxing to me to think about giving up things I love. I felt very anxious during the exercise and felt myself not wanting to think about these things.'' Keep in mind that resistance is a defense mechanism which enables participants to retain control of their experience, and thus should be respected.

This exercise is interspersed with a number of writing assignments for the participants. Tell them in advance about that and be sure that all are supplied with pen and paper. Make sure that you allow participants sufficient time to complete the assignments you give them. If time is limited, shorten the list of things which they are to surrender.

### Guided Imagery

Get as comfortable as you can in the chair in which you are sitting . . . Uncross your arms and legs and let gravity have its way with your body . . . letting your body sink into the chair . . . trusting the chair to sustain your weight . . . letting your body relax from its regular chore of holding you erect and keeping you prepared for action . . . As your body becomes more and more relaxed, let go of the tensions and worries that have been close to the surface of your consciousness . . . letting them fly away like birds that have been freed from a cage . . . becoming aware of how much more relaxed and peaceful you feel as you release the tension in your muscles and quiet your nerves . . . letting your breathing come more slowly . . . letting the inner stillness wrap itself around your soul . . . letting your inner self match the rhythm of your breathing . . . breathing in . . . and breathing out . . . breathing in . . . and breathing out . . . feeling your worries and tensions flowing out of you as you exhale, and feeling the spirit of God filling you each time you inhale . . . tensions flowing out as the breath flows out . . . the Spirit of God flowing in as the breath flows in . . . breathing in . . . and breathing out . . . breathing in . . . and breathing out.

Jesus says: "Whoever would save his life will lose it; and whoever loses his life for my sake and the Gospel's will save it." Let your mind drift back over the years and try to recall three or four different occasions when you were aware of letting go of something important to you—not because you had to, as when someone dies, but because you chose to even if the loss of control was very hard. It may have been an occasion when you surrendered your pride and acknowledged a deep wrong that you had done to another. It may have been an occasion when you gave up a relationship that had been very important to you but that you could not continue. It may have been an occasion when you gave up something important to you for the sake of another person, perhaps a bad habit. It may be something you gave up because it was bad for you, like smoking. Or something you gave up for the Lenten season. As you remember times when you let go of something that you valued, jot them down with a word or a phrase, just enough to help you remember the occasion you are thinking of, and then close your eyes again to search the past for other occasions. (Pause for 2–3 minutes)

After you have identified three or four such occasions, choose one that you would like to reflect on more deeply. With the aid of your imagination go back to that time and reenter that experience. What were the circumstances surrounding the event? Who else was involved? Was there one special person? Picture the persons who were involved exactly as you remember them. What was it that you let go of? What was it that you risked in letting go? What was the hardest thing for you about letting go? Did your letting go leave you vulnerable? How so? What were the consequences of letting go? Did that make it harder or easier to let go after that? Do you wish now that you could change what happened or would you do it again just as it happened? As you are ready, write what you are feeling and thinking. Try to stay within the experience while you are writing, opening your eyes just enough to let your pen record what you are experiencing within the center of yourself. (Allow 5–10 minutes for writing)

As you put your pen aside, let that past experience go, close your eyes once more, and return to the quiet of your inner self. Within the quiet of that inner space reflect on those things you value most in your life right now and make a list of those things on the left-hand side of your paper. Be spontaneous in your choices, trusting that your intuition will be right in its selections. Do not include your faith or God on this list since your faith is a resource that enables you to let go of those things which are not at the center of your life. Stop when you've reached six items on your list of things that are of value to you. (Pause for 1–2 minutes)

After you have made six choices, list them in the order of their importance in a column on the right from one to six. Don't question why you feel that one choice is more important than another. Your feelings are a better guide than a calculated judgment that may prompt you to choose what you think *should* be important. **(Pause for 2–3 minutes)**

After you've numbered your choices, look at the sixth choice and once again close your eyes. Let an image form in your mind of whatever that is. After that image is formed in your mind, make a conscious choice to let it go and then do so—by giving whatever it is to another person or to God, or by turning and walking away, or by watching what you have let go vanish from your mind's eye. **(Pause for 1–2 minutes)** Do the same for what is fifth on your list, and fourth, and third, and second, and finally the last and most important item on your list. Be sure you take the time to form a mental image of every item on your list and then let it go without feeling hurried. You will likely experience increasing resistance as you get to the top items on your list. **(Pause for 5–10 minutes)**

What does it feel like to have surrendered the six most important things in your life? What was the hardest thing for you in letting go of what is important? Did you reach a point where you found it too hard to go on? Are there some things that you could never willingly surrender? For example, can you imagine willingly letting go of your life? Was that on the list of things you wrote down? If not, imagine now what it would be like to let your life go rather than having it ripped away from you as you try to hang on to it. **(Pause for 1–2 minutes)** What is it that enables you to let go or keeps you from letting go? What would you need to do in order to make it easier in the future to let go? Express what you think and feel on paper, but do not judge or criticize anything that wells up from the inner world of your thoughts and feelings. **(Allow 15–20 minutes for writing)**

## LUKE 23:44–46  ◇  Were You There When They Crucified My Lord?

*Notes for the Leader*

Both structured and unstructured forms of this exercise are provided. The first part of the script is the same for both. There are advantages and disadvantages to both options. The advantage to the structured form is that you as the leader can direct the experience along a path that you choose, e.g., guiding people through an experience of being present when Jesus died and making the link between his death and theirs. The disadvantage to the more structured form of the exercise is that you are asking people to experience an actual event that is distant in the past and loaded with doctrinal content and sermonic overlays. Furthermore, one can anticipate some resistance because the scene of the crucifixion is not a comfortable place to be. The advantage to the unstructured form of the exercise is that it creates an aura of mystery for a meditation on the meaning of the cross that can be a fertile ground for the spawning of images which are true to the experience of each individual participant.

Both the structured and unstructured forms of the exercise are relatively short and can be done within twenty minutes. A guided imagery meditation on the cross can be particularly effective in a worship setting, perhaps as a substitute for a homily at a Lenten service. If used in this way, the portion of the exercise that takes place within a cathedral could be eliminated or adapted to the setting within which the service is taking place.

The purpose of this exercise should be explained beforehand unless the context makes it obvious, e.g., a Lenten meditation or a sermon on the crucifixion. Rather than words about Christ's death and its meaning for our life and death, this exercise is designed to help people be there with the aid of their imagination. The purpose is not to focus attention on feelings of pity, anger, or remorse that might be aroused through such an experience, but to facilitate a faith-filled response to the death of Jesus at a deeper-than-intellectual level. Make that point clear as you introduce this exercise in order to avoid sentimentality and to help people focus on faith issues. It is not necessary to read the story of the crucifixion since it is so well known. A few verses from Luke 23 are sufficient to introduce the guided imagery:

> It was now about the sixth hour, and there was darkness over the whole land until the ninth hour, while the sun's light failed; and the curtain of the temple was torn in two. Then Jesus, crying with a loud voice, said, "Father, into thy hands I commit my spirit!" And having said this he breathed his last.

### Guided Imagery

Stretch your muscles and let them relax. Pay attention to places in your body where you may feel tension—perhaps in your neck, or stomach, or back. Tense the muscles in that region and let them relax . . .

Close your eyes in order to see what's going on inside of you rather than having all your attention focused on what's going on outside of you. Concentrate on your breathing and its natural rhythm until your whole being is in tune with that rhythm . . . breathing in . . . and breathing out . . . breathing in fresh energy and vitality . . . breathing out tension and weariness . . . sitting in silence . . . breathing in and out from the center of your being . . . waiting calmly for what is to be revealed to you from the Spirit of God who dwells within the depths of your human spirit.

As you wait, you find yourself in a great cathedral, a cathedral with rich stained glass windows which take your breath away. It is quiet in the darkened cathedral, which is lit only by the subdued light from the stained glass windows. You can feel a powerful presence in this place, a presence that exudes beauty and majesty and power. At the far end of the cathedral you can see an altar, and behind the altar a cross. As you walk to the front of the cathedral you can see that there is a figure on the cross shaped in the form of the *Christus Rex* (Christ the King). It is Jesus on the cross with arms outstretched in a gesture of victory rather than being slumped over in a posture of defeat, and on his head is the crown of a king rather than a crown of thorns. As you reach the front of the cathedral, you sit in one of the pews, keeping your eyes fixed on the cross, meditating on its meaning for your living and your dying.

Meditating on the cross in the midst of the darkened cathedral and its silent witness to a God of power and majesty . . . resting quietly in the center of yourself, you are aware of the presence of the Spirit of God within you, waiting calmly in the center of yourself, feeling the rhythm of your steady, even breathing.

### (OPTION 1—Structured Meditation)

As the stillness and calm deepen within you, your imagination carries you back over time to the first century, to the time when Jesus was alive, to the time when he died. You find it easy to do because the story is so familiar to you and because the setting of the darkened cathedral invites such reflection. In your mind's eye imagine yourself approaching the Mount of Calvary from within the city of ancient Jerusalem. You can just barely make out three crosses standing upon a hill. You are aware of the distance that separates you and the cross of Jesus. He seems far away, as far away as he sometimes feels when you are sitting in a pew and hearing about his death. With the aid of your imagination you are able to eliminate that distance as you walk slowly through the streets of Jerusalem toward the Mount of Calvary just beyond the outskirts of the city. The streets are crowded with people engaged in their usual activities, equally oblivious of you and of Jesus. You are at the outskirts of the city now, slowly making your way up the side of the hill, side-by-side with others who are curious. As you come nearer and nearer to the place of his crucifixion, let yourself blend quite naturally into the scene, one among many who are there to witness the dying of Jesus.

Use all the powers of your imagination to enter fully into that experience. Picture in your mind's eye the three crosses, two thieves on either side of Jesus, the Roman soldiers in charge, the bystanders—some there to taunt him and others to comfort him. Hear the sounds of the soldiers arguing over the robe of Jesus, laughing among themselves. Hear the jeers of those who taunt him and the words of comfort from those, mostly women, who would console him. Smell the sweat, the vinegar, the dust.

Now let your attention be focused on Jesus. Let the full realism of his dying permeate your consciousness: the pain, the suffering, the loneliness, the helplessness, the forsakenness. Hear the words which he speaks: words of forgiveness for those who put him to death, words that express the dreadful isolation and God-forsakenness that he felt, words of physical suffering, words of caring for his mother, words of spiritual suffering and surrender. As you stand beneath the cross, the light begins to fade as if it were dusk until the whole scene is shrouded in darkness. Silence settles upon the crowd as the darkness deepens, a silence finally broken by a soul-piercing cry: "It is finished!"—and then after a moment . . . another, more subdued voice that you recognize as coming from the centurion who commands the Roman troops: "Surely this was the Son of God!" **(Pause for 30 seconds)**

In your mind's eye picture a shaft of light piercing the darkness, illuminating only the cross. And what you see are the arms of Christ outstretched in victory and the crown of a king upon his head. As your eyes are focused on that vision, feel the sign of the cross being made on your forehead and hear the words "dead" and "risen" spoken directly to you by a voice from you know not where. Let the distance between you and Jesus on the cross diminish until in your mind's eye you see yourself as cruciform so that the dying of Jesus is at the same time your dying, and feel yourself being transformed by a transcendent power from beyond the grave so that his rising from the dead is your rising as well. Feel yourself at one with him who died and rose again, and let the richness of that experience fill your whole being.

As you feel ready, express what you feel and think in writing, letting the pen be the medium of your inner self. Write spontaneously, without judgment or criticism. **(Allow 15–20 minutes for writing)**

### (OPTION 2—Unstructured Meditation)

As the stillness and calm deepen within you, you find yourself in a forest with trees so tall that they seem to reach to the sky. The branches of the trees, high above you, provide a covering that looks like the vaulted ceiling of a cathedral. The bright sun cannot reach the cool forest floor where you walk with bare feet on lush green grass fed by an underground spring. There is quiet and a peaceful calm all around you as you walk in the lush grass of the forest floor.

Feeling the mystery of the forest cathedral through which you walk on a path that takes you ever deeper into its center, you come across a small clearing in the forest. Though the deep shade makes it difficult to see clearly, you are able to make out two huge beams which are in the form of a cross at the center of the clearing. Awed by the size of the beams and the majesty of the setting, you are drawn to the foot of the cross.

You are standing at the foot of the cross deep in the forest. It is dark at the floor of the forest, except for a soft light that seems to emanate from the cross which towers above you. The soft quality of the light is calming and quieting and assuring. In the light you feel a power and a presence that is both in and beyond the light, a presence that does not diminish, a light that enables you to see the cross more clearly and feel its presence more powerfully.

As the experience deepens, reflect on what comes to you from within the experience about the mystery of the cross. Standing at the foot of the mighty cross at the center of the forest, you feel a power and a presence both in and beyond the light. A voice is heard in the stillness of the forest only by you with the ears of your inner self. Filled with a sense of awe and mystery at being in this holy place, you listen carefully to the voice which speaks out of the silence only to you. Let the experience deepen. . . . As you feel ready, express in writing what comes to you from within the experience about the mystery of the cross.

## MATTHEW 25:31-46 ◇ Before the Judgment Seat

*Notes for the Leader*

For fully half of the two thousand years of recorded Christian history, the primary image of death has been an image of judgment. It was with fear and trembling that Christians contemplated the day of judgment when their souls would be weighed on the scales of justice. Demons tempted the dying and waited anxiously to pounce on the soul as it departed the body. Even if one were fortunate enough to escape the fires of hell, a person's soul would still need at least to be purged of its remaining evil before dwelling in the presence of a holy God.

We no longer live with the same kind of fear of judgment that characterized the medieval period of Christian history, but guilt is still a fundamental dynamic of Christian consciousness. The purpose of this exercise is to give expression to the feelings of guilt and the fear of judgment which are an inevitable part of our relationship to God. The judgment we fear is death, eternal death. The guilt we feel is evidence that we deserve this judgment. This dimension of our relationship to God, no matter how negative the feelings it evokes, needs to be faced with the confidence that nothing can separate us from the love of God in Christ.

Jesus' parable of the last judgment contains well-known imagery of the judgment of God at the time of death. Though it is familiar, I would urge that the parable be read before beginning the guided imagery.

### Guided Imagery

Letting the self become still . . . letting the tension fade away . . . letting tranquility flood the mind . . . letting the breathing become even and slow . . . sitting in quietness with eyes closed . . . waiting for the muddiness in the water of our lives to settle. As the waters become quiet and clear, as the inner awareness deepens, as the heart yearns for understanding, the moment of revelation is near. Let the breathing come evenly and deeply as you wait in silence. The waters are clear now and quiet . . . transparent as you look into them . . . quiet as a still lake which mirrors the environment around it. Looking into the quiet waters which are you . . . waiting for images to appear that will reveal what is within . . . looking deeply within yourself for a clear picture of yourself as others see you, as God sees you, as you in your most open and vulnerable moments see yourself.

In your mind's eye imagine yourself seated on a hard-backed chair in the middle of a room. Surrounding you on every side are tiered rows of seats filled with people who have known you, plus some who are strangers. All of those present have needed you in some way. Some have asked for your help and some have not. Some have received what they needed from you, but others have not. Some are hungry. Some are poor. Some are emotionally starved. Some are very young. Some are very old. The number is very great, so many people who have needed so much from you.

As you sit in this room with all eyes focused on you, one of this array of needy people comes forward and sits directly in front of you. It is somebody you know. Let the image of that person form in your mind as he or she approaches. This person looks directly into your eyes and tells you what he or she needed from you that you were never able or willing to give. Listen carefully to what is being said as you look directly into the eyes of the person who is speaking. Do not attempt to defend yourself or offer excuses. Simply listen to what is being said. **(Pause for 1 minute)** After having listened carefully to what this person has needed but not received, let the image of that person fade away and be replaced by an image of Jesus sitting in front of you. Let the image form spontaneously in any way that seems natural to you. Look closely at the face of Jesus for the expression that you find there. What do you see in his eyes? Disappointment? Judgment? Compassion? Perhaps a mingling of all those expressions and more?

Now let another person come forward, this time someone who is a stranger to you. Let an image of a stranger who may have needed you take shape in your mind. He or she takes the chair directly in front of you. Let the image form spontaneously without forcing it. What does this stranger look like? How old is the person? How is he or she dressed? Don't second-guess your choice of images. Simply let the image take shape in any form that your inner consciousness suggests. As this stranger sits across from you and looks directly into your eyes, listen carefully to what this person tells you about what he or she needed from you that you were not willing or able to give. Listen carefully to what is being said as you look directly into the eyes of the person who is speaking. Do not attempt to defend yourself or offer excuses. Simply listen to what is being said. **(Pause for 1 minute)** Having listened carefully to what this person has needed but not received, let the image of that person fade away and be replaced by the image of Jesus sitting in front of you. Look closely at the face of Jesus for the expression that you find there. **(Pause for 30 seconds)**

As you remain seated in the same chair, the room around you is transformed. All the people are gone, and the room is empty. There is no door. There are no windows. The room is brightly lit, but there is no obvious source of the light. The walls, the ceiling, and the floor are all mirrors. No matter where you look, you see a reflection of yourself. You look to the right and then to the left; you look up and then down—only to see images of yourself from different perspectives, images reflected over and over again so that the whole room is filled with images of you. Take a moment to experience what it is like to be in a room where there is no escape from images of yourself. **(Pause for 1 minute)**

Now recall a time when you were feeling very bad about yourself, but instead of being judged you received an act of kindness from another, an act that you could never deserve or expect, much less ask for. Recall the circumstances around that event and with the aid of your imagination reenter the experience. Recall in as much detail as you can what it was that made you feel so badly about yourself. What did the person do that helped you to feel better about yourself? Feel the goodness of being cared for when you expected only judgment and criticism. Now let the image of that person fade from your mind and be replaced by an image of a forgiving God. Let yourself feel the full weight of your sinfulness and then let images of God's forgiveness flood your mind. There may be many images—images which come from the Bible, images which come from your experience, images which come from stories you've heard. . . . Select one of those images and let it form fully in your mind. **(Pause for 4–5 minutes)**

Now let the image shift once more, this time to the scene of the last judgment. You are a part of a vast throng of people surrounding the judgment seat of Christ. Where do you see yourself in this crowd and what do you expect to hear from Jesus? Let that drama unfold of its own accord as you watch it being projected on the screen of your mind's eye. Let it unfold spontaneously without any effort on your part to direct it or change it. **(Pause for 3–4 minutes)**

As you feel ready, write what you feel and think as you reflect on the experience of being judged and still loved and cared for without reservation or condition. **(Allow 10–15 minutes for writing)**

### REVELATION 21:1–4  ◇  Heaven—Unending Hope and Fulfillment

*Notes to the Leader*

Nowhere is imagery more needed or more suspect than in relation to heaven. It is needed because the biblical images we have and the ones we create are our only way of anticipating the fullness of life which God intends for us in heaven. It is suspect because imaging, like every other human activity, can be put in the service of a hedonistic and narcissistic ego just as easily as it can be put in the service of faith.

St. Paul comes down on the side of caution. He is clear and explicit in his statements **that** there is eternal life, but cautious in saying **what** that is. His summary statement is: "If we live, we live to the Lord, and if we die we die to the Lord; so then, whether we live or whether we die, we are the Lord's" (Rom 14:8). Though he seems to have had a glimpse of heaven, all we have from him is a negative description of it: "What no eye has seen, nor ear heard, nor the heart of man conceived, what God has prepared for those who love him" (1 Cor 2:9).

Lest we become too cautious, however, we need to be reminded that Jesus makes ready use of imagery in depicting the joys of heaven, the bread of eternal life, an everlasting spring of water, nets filled to bursting, precious pearls, a wedding feast, a hundredfold harvest. In the Revelation of John the imagery is even more extravagant. The elect are comforted by the wiping away of their tears. There is no more death or pain, no hunger or thirst.

I have devoted more space than usual to these introductory notes in order to provide biblical warrant for engaging in an exercise in guided imagery on what we might call the "completion" of our being in heaven. Through all of life we project images of fulfillment onto the future. It can be something as simple as the completion of a task. It can be something as complicated as marriage and a family. The need for imaging a tangible future does not end at death. Mary Austin, the nineteenth century American author, once said that she was not afraid of death as "extinction," but death as a future state in which she would find herself stripped of her "dearest purchase of living." Heaven as an abstract concept does not satisfy the need for some form of continuity between life as experienced in the present and life as it will unfold in the future.

For those who have some reservations about the use of imagery in relation to something that can only be imagined, as St. Paul apparently did, this exercise may simply be ignored. If the exercise is being done in a group, the leader should note the differences in the use of imagery by Paul, John, and Jesus, allowing individuals to decide for themselves about the limits and possibilities of their own use of imagery.

Note that there are two different exercises for imagining heaven, each to be used separately on different occasions. The same introduction is used for both exercises. I would encourage you to read Revelation 21:1–4 prior to the beginning of either exercise even though there are no specific references to the passage in either exercise. Indicate to the participants that they will be asked to list certain experiences during the exercise and encourage them to remain in the experiential mode of being while they do this.

### Guided Imagery—First Exercise

Get as comfortable as you can in the chair on which you are seated. Uncross your arms and legs. Close your eyes, and as the quietness deepens within yourself, let your breathing come more slowly . . . letting the tenseness in your body drain away . . . letting the stillness enter your soul . . . letting the breath come more slowly . . . feeling the movement of life—bursting from the womb, growing, developing, leaning into the world . . . sensing the wonder of life as it moves through its phases . . . and passages . . . and cycles . . . flowing down the stream of life . . . flowing past markers for each of the years . . . observing milestones along the way . . . moving faster and faster as the stream of life flows on . . . seeking truth and meaning in the stream of my life . . . remembering and wondering and yearning as the stream of life moves on . . . remembering the deep gladness of years past . . . wondering where the stream of life will lead . . . yearning for the fulfillment of my being . . . yearning for a becoming that has no end.

As you enter fully the stream of life that is you, identify the longings within yourself that have been and continue to be closest to the center of the real you, the longings which prompt you to say, "This is really important. This should not be lost. This is representative of the best in me." As you identify such longings in yourself, jot down a word or phrase which captures the sense of it. It might be a physical longing for success in a favorite sport. It might be an aesthetic yearning to create a beautiful work of art or a musical composition. It might be a yearning for a deeper level of intimacy with a person who is very important to you. It might be a yearning for a truth of which you've only had glimpses. It might be a yearning for peace in a world embroiled in conflict. Identify six to eight such yearnings in your soul and make note of them. Open your eyes long enough and wide enough to jot down a word or phrase so that you can remain within the world of your inner experience. (Pause for 2–3 minutes)

After you have made your selection, look over the list and select one of them for further reflection. It need not be the most important one if you were ordering them on a scale of values. Choose the one which is the most interesting, which generates the most energy in you. (Pause for 30 seconds)

Having made a selection of a yearning within you that you are ready to reflect on more deeply, close your eyes and enter that yearning. Become one with that yearning until you and the yearning are the same. Let that yearning take you wherever it would go. What would it be like for that longing to be fulfilled? Within your imagination experience the fulfillment of your longing. Let the experience unfold naturally and spontaneously. Don't attempt to direct it according to preconceived notions of what it will be. Simply be the yearning and go where it takes you. Imagine that you are inside a dream of your own making, a waking dream that opens up a future that could only be experienced in dreamlike images. Experience the fulfillment of your longing without the longing itself being extinguished. (Pause for 2–3 minutes)

As you feel ready, write what you are feeling and thinking as you experience in your imagination what heaven will be like for you. Let your writing be an expression of what you are feeling and thinking rather than a commentary about it. Stay as close to the imagery as you can, letting the pen be the voice of your inner self.

## Guided Imagery—Second Exercise

Get as comfortable as you can in the chair on which you are seated. Uncross your arms and legs. Close your eyes, and as the quietness deepens within yourself, let your breathing come more slowly . . . letting the tenseness in your body drain away . . . letting the stillness enter your soul . . . letting the breath come more slowly . . . feeling the movement of life—bursting from the womb, growing, developing, leaning into the world . . . sensing the wonder of life as it moves through its phases . . . and passages . . . and cycles . . . flowing down the stream of life . . . flowing past markers for each of the years . . . observing milestones along the way . . . moving faster and faster as the stream of life flows on . . . seeking truth and meaning in the stream of my life . . . remembering and wondering and yearning as the stream of life moves on . . . remembering the deep gladness of years past . . . wondering where the stream of life will lead . . . yearning for the fulfillment of my being . . . yearning for a becoming that has no end.

As you enter fully into the stream of life that is you, identify peak experiences that you have had as a Christian, experiences of spiritual fulfillment, experiences when you have had an especially keen sense of your identity as a child of God. List six to eight such experiences with the use of a word or a phrase that you associate with that experience. It might be a milestone event in your Christian life such as baptism, or First Communion, or confirmation. It might have been an experience of wonder at the marvels of God's creation—a sunset, a snow-capped mountain, the Grand Canyon. It might have been an experience of worship— receiving the body and blood of Christ, a candlelight service, a triumphant Easter hymn or song. It might have been a musical experience, such as hearing or singing Handel's Messiah or Bach's B Minor Mass. It might have been a visit to a great cathedral, like Notre Dame, or viewing a great work of art, like Michelangelo's fresco of the creation on the ceiling of the Sistine Chapel. List six to eight such peak experiences in your life as a Christian. Open your eyes just long enough to write down a word or a phrase. **(Pause for 2–3 minutes)**

After you have selected six to eight such experiences, look over the list and choose one of them for further reflection. Choose the one which generates the strongest feelings. **(Pause for 30 seconds)** With the aid of your memory and your imagination, go back to that experience and reenter it. Remember it with your whole being and not just your intellect. How old were you when you had this experience? Were you alone or was there someone there to share it with you? Picture the setting in your mind's eye. Hear the sounds that are there—the words, the music, the background noises. Experience everything that surrounds you. What is that you are feeling? How do you experience the presence of God in the place where you find yourself? Do you experience him as close or as distant, as loving or as aloof, as powerful or as weak? What makes this such a special experience for you? Has there ever been an experience like it or was it unique? Can you imagine a time when such an experience would be as common as eating and sleeping?

As you feel ready, use this peak experience of your Christian life as a way of imagining what heaven will be like. Begin your writing with the words: "Heaven will be like . . . **(Allow 15–20 minutes for writing)**

# 8. In Anticipation of Dying

All of the exercises in Chapters 6 and 7 use scriptural passages as a point of departure. The exercises in Chapters 8, 9 and 10 are designed for special purposes. The focus in this chapter is anticipation of dying.

The exercises in this chapter are designed primarily for those who have no immediate prospect of dying but are looking for ways to prepare themselves for it and integrate the reality of their dying into their present experience. Isn't this a dangerous thing to do in a death-denying culture? Is it possible that a person's defenses might be bypassed through an exercise like this with the consequence that he or she is overwhelmed by a flood of anxiety that cannot be controlled? My experience in the use of this exercise and others like it suggests the opposite. Death anxiety is eased through imagery of one's own death, not heightened. Furthermore, needed defenses remain intact. There is no intrusive probing with guided imagery. Each person is in full control of the experience, choosing the images which are appropriate to her, and determining the level of involvement in the experience. This might mean that a person with a high level of death anxiety will discover that the imagery exercise simply doesn't work—images do not appear, the mind wanders, and relaxation leads to drowsiness rather than heightened inner awareness.

Should you tell participants in advance what to expect from exercises that anticipate their dying? The answer to that question varies from exercise to exercise, and I will make recommendations in "Notes for the Leader" preceding each exercise. It is assumed that participants will know in advance that the exercise is in the general topic area of death and dying, but they do not specifically need to know the content of a particular exercise in order to prepare themselves emotionally for it. All of the feedback which I have received supports my contention that you do not need to fear that participants will be overwhelmed with anxiety by an exercise in which they anticipate their dying. They do find the experience very realistic, but they are also able to make clear distinctions between the imaginary and the real.

## DYING I

*Notes for the Leader*

The feedback which I have received from doing this exercise suggests that most participants feel that the exercise is more realistic and their reactions more spontaneous if they are not told what to expect. Though some said it makes no difference, nobody said that it would be better to know beforehand.

It is especially important in these exercises to allow participants sufficient time to process their experience during the exercise. Don't rush! You are asking the participants to do something that they have probably never done before, and they need time to experience it fully. Pay special attention to this in the last part of the exercise where you are directed to ask a series of thought-provoking questions. Pause long enough for the question to have been heard and briefly considered at the deeper level of their being. Some people will object to the writing which they are asked to do in the middle of the exercise because they find it difficult to write while in a more meditative, experiential mode of being, but I think it is helpful to have a longer and deeper period of reflection after the experience of speaking to someone about the news that death is imminent.

This exercise will likely prompt the participants to be more reflective about their own death. Some of those people (not all) would benefit from an opportunity to share their experience. Sharing with another person who has just completed the exercise or allowing people who wish to read what they have written does not have the same level of threat as a therapeutic setting because full control is still retained by the individual who had the experience. If this exercise is done in a group setting, individuals can be given the opportunity to share what they wish with the person next to them or read aloud what they have written without others commenting on it or asking questions. The leader of the group might also offer to meet privately with individuals who wish to talk more about what they have experienced.

### *Guided Imagery*

Stretch your arms and legs. Rotate your head to relieve the tension in the muscles of your neck. Move your shoulders up and around. As you ease the tension in these muscles, you will feel your whole body relax. Settle yourself as comfortably as you can in your chair with your arms and legs uncrossed. Close your eyes, letting gravity have its way with your body . . . letting the tensions drain away . . . feeling more and more at peace with yourself . . . becoming more aware of your breathing as it moves in and out . . . quietly and steadily . . . breathing in . . . and breathing out . . . steadily and quietly . . . breathing in energy and life . . . breathing out tension and distress . . . breathing in . . . and breathing out . . . steadily and quietly . . . taking in energy and life . . . letting go of tension and distress . . . breathing in . . . and breathing out . . . steadily and quietly . . . letting the stillness in the room radiate to the center of your soul . . . concentrating only on breathing in and breathing out . . . steadily and quietly . . . feeling the goodness of being alive . . . breathing in the breath of life . . . breathing in the breath of God . . . steadily and quietly. How easy and natural the breathing . . . the breathing in . . . and breathing out . . . feeling the wonder of the gift of life . . . the gift of breathing . . . breathing in . . . and breathing out . . . steadily and quietly.

With the aid of your imagination picture yourself in the office of your physician. You are there because you have not been feeling well—unexplained tiredness, poor appetite and loss of weight, a persistent cough that won't go away. You've undergone a series of tests and a thorough examination by the physician, and you are there to get the results. As you sit in the doctor's office, you hear your physician informing you that you have an acute form of leukemia that will likely end your life within six months. With treatment life expectancy might be extended to two years. Let a clear image of the doctor form in your mind. Look for the facial expression in his or her face. Pay attention to the tone of voice as well as the content of what he or she is saying to you. As you listen, what are the feelings deep inside yourself? What is your initial reaction to hearing this news? Allow yourself time to let what the doctor is saying sink in and then when you are ready write down some words and phrases, not full sentences, to capture the felt sense of your immediate response, opening your eyes just enough to jot down what you are feeling and thinking. **(Pause for 2–3 minutes)**

Imagine yourself leaving the doctor's office. Having heard the news of your impending death, where will you go? With whom do you wish to talk? What do you say? Let yourself spontaneously choose where you would like to go and to whom you would like to talk. It might be to a church to talk to God. Or perhaps the home of a good friend or family member. You may wish to talk to a priest or pastor, or even someone you don't know well or don't even know at all, but a person you feel close to from what you've heard or read. Imagine what you would say to this person and what you would like to hear in return.

Knowing that you are in the presence of someone who understands you and is worthy of your trust, pour out some of your feelings and thoughts about God, about yourself, about your relationships, about what's really important to you as you think about the nearness of your death. He or she is a good listener, giving you permission to say exactly what you feel. As you begin to express yourself, let your pen be the means by which those feelings and thoughts are recorded. **(Allow 10–15 minutes for writing)**

The time of your death is rapidly approaching. Imagine yourself being very, very sick. Let images of yourself in progressive stages of physical deterioration form in your mind's eye until there is radical loss of weight, a worn and haggard face which appears older than your natural age. Imagine yourself looking into a mirror and being shocked by what you see. The reality of the irreversible process of the disease hits you as it had not before. Experience the feelings and thoughts which accompany the process of realizing your movement toward the end-stages of your dying. What seems important to you at this point? Would you want to be alone or with others? How would you want to spend your time? **(Pause for 2–3 minutes)**

Imagine yourself now in a hospice or a hospital, or a room in your home that has been equipped with everything necessary to meet your physical needs in the last days of your life. Furnish the room in any way that you wish. Make it large enough to accommodate as many people as you would wish to be present. Aware that you are living the last days and hours of your life, what is it that you need most at this time? . . . Whom would you like to be taking care of you? . . . Choose some of the people that you would like to be there. . . . What do you need from them more than anything else in these last days of your life? . . . How easy would it be for you to ask for the help you need? . . . How ready would you be to receive the help that they would offer you? . . . What would be the hardest part of the experience of these last days? . . . What would give you the greatest feeling of comfort and assurance? . . . Would faith be an important resource for you? . . . Would you expect

or want others to pray with you? . . . to read to you from the Bible? . . .
As you feel ready, let the experience of these last days find expression
in your writing. **(Allow 15–20 minutes for writing)**

## DYING II

*Notes for the Leader*
   The purpose of this exercise is the same as for "Dying I." Before
doing this exercise, read the "Notes to the Leader" for that exercise because they apply to this exercise as well.
   The first two paragraphs of each of these exercises is the same. In
each one the person is told by his physician that death is imminent.
"Dying I" focuses on how that individual copes with the news and follows the progressive course of the disease. "Dying II" focuses on how
a person deals with important relationships in the light of this news.
   In this exercise the participants will be asked to choose five people
with whom they will share the news of their dying. This comes fairly
easily to most people because they have already thought about this frequently. Do not presume that you know the choices people will make,
e.g., "You will, of course, want to include members of your family."
One person chose a two-year-old to tell first. There are reasons why people make the choices they do, including the need for necessary defenses.
For example, it may seem too hard to face a spouse or a child with such
news. Whatever the reason for the choices made, it should be respected.
   A large number of respondents to both this and the previous exercise report some denial while being told of their impending death, e.g.,
"I could tell that half of me didn't believe him." The explanation is not
inadequate imagery, but resistance, e.g., "I tried to find humor in what
the doctor was saying." Such denial is normal.
   The full realization of their dying is more likely to come for participants in that part of the exercise where they tell others, but many report
that this conversation is more painful for the ones being told than it is
for them. This part of the exercise is likely to be very powerful. Some
report surprise at how important some relationships are. Others report
that they didn't know the people with whom they spoke as well as they
thought. Though the encounters brought few genuine surprises, almost
all report a deepening and enriching of their awareness of important people in their lives.

## *Guided Imagery*

Stretch your arms and legs. Rotate your head to relieve the tension in the muscles of your neck. Move your shoulders up and around. As you ease the tension in these muscles, you will feel your whole body relax. Settle yourself as comfortably as you can in your chair with your arms and legs uncrossed. Close your eyes, letting gravity have its way with your body . . . letting the tensions drain away . . . feeling more and more at peace with yourself . . . becoming more aware of your breathing as it moves in and out . . . quietly and steadily . . . breathing in . . . and breathing out . . . steadily and quietly . . . breathing in energy and life . . . breathing out tension and distress . . . breathing in . . . and breathing out . . . steadily and quietly . . . taking in energy and life . . . letting go of tension and distress . . . breathing in . . . and breathing out . . . steadily and quietly . . . letting the stillness in the room radiate to the center of your soul . . . concentrating only on breathing in and breathing out . . . steadily and quietly . . . feeling the goodness of being alive . . . breathing in the breath of life . . . breathing in the breath of God . . . steadily and quietly. How easy and natural the breathing . . . the breathing in . . . and breathing out . . . feeling the wonder of the gift of life . . . the gift of breathing . . . breathing in . . . and breathing out . . . steadily and quietly.

With the aid of your imagination picture yourself in the office of your physician. You are there because you have not been feeling well—unexplained tiredness, poor appetite and loss of weight, a persistent cough that won't go away. You've undergone a series of tests and a thorough examination by the physician, and you are there to get the results. As you sit in the doctor's office, you hear your physician informing you that you have an acute form of leukemia that will likely end your life within six months. With treatment life expectancy might be extended to two years. Let a clear image of the doctor form in your mind. Look for the facial expression in his or her face. Pay attention to the tone of voice as well as the content of what he or she is saying to you. As you listen, what are the feelings deep inside yourself? What is your initial reaction to hearing this news? Allow yourself time to let what the doctor is saying sink in and then when you are ready write down some words and phrases, not full sentences, to capture the felt sense of your immediate response, opening your eyes just enough to jot down what you are feeling and thinking. **(Pause for 2–3 minutes)**

As you leave the doctor's office, begin to reflect on some of the people who will be affected by your death. There are too many for you to consider them all, so limit yourself to a selection of five with whom you would want to share the news of your terminal illness. In some cases, like immediate family or grandparents, you may wish to tell them at the same time. As the names of those individuals or small groups come to you, jot them down on the left side of the paper in front of you. They don't need to be in order of importance. You may be surprised at some of the names that come to you; don't let your surprise keep you from putting the name down. The only basis for deciding should be: "I want him or her to know." **(Pause for 2–3 minutes)**

After you have made your selection of five, look over the list and decide which of the persons should be told first, which second, etc., until the list has been reordered and rewritten. **(Pause for 1 minute)**

Begin with the name at the top of the list. With your eyes closed, imagine the person sitting or standing directly in front of you. The location can be in your home or anyplace else where you can be assured of privacy. You have arranged this meeting, saying that you had something important to share, and so he or she is waiting expectantly. In whatever way seems appropriate to you, tell the person about the diagnosis of terminal illness and observe the expression on his or her face as you do so. **(Pause for 30 seconds)** Now listen to what he or she has to tell you in return. **(Pause for 1 minute)**

Take the opportunity to tell this person what you think is important for him or her to hear from you about the importance of this relationship to you and what your hopes and wishes are for this person in the future. **(Pause for 1 minute)** Listen to what he or she has to say to you in return. **(Pause for 1 minute)** Take your leave of this person in whatever way seems appropriate to you. **(Pause for 1 minute)**

Choose the second person on your list and tell him or her about your impending death, observing the expression on his or her face as you do so. **(Pause for 30 seconds)** Now listen to what he or she has to tell you in return. **(Pause for 1 minute)** Take the opportunity to tell this person what you think is important for him or her to hear from you about the importance of this relationship to you and what your hopes and wishes are for this person in the future. **(Pause for 1 minute)** Listen to what he or she has to say to you in return. **(Pause for 1 minute)** Take your leave of this person in whatever way seems appropriate to you. **(Pause for 1 minute)**

Repeat the same procedure with the remaining persons on your list. **(Pause for 10 minutes)**

**(Note: Writing is optional for this exercise. If it is included, introduce it in the following way:)**

After you have finished saying goodbye to the five people on your list, write a few sentences about your relationship to each of them, beginning with the words: "The changes that I would like to make in my relationship to **(name)** in the future are. . . ."

Repeat the same procedure with the second person on the list. Do as many of the people on the list as you can in the time allotted. Begin each one of them with the words: "The changes that I would like to make in my relationship to **(name)** in the future are . . . **(Allow 15–20 minutes for writing)**

## DIALOGUE WITH YOUR DYING

*Notes for the Leader*

The exercises in this chapter call for the imaging of one's own dying. The two previous exercises, "DYING I" and "DYING II," are highly structured; specific images are suggested in order to provide a particular kind of experience. The following exercise is different from those in that it is more unstructured and personal. Each person will draw on her own life-history in constructing this experience. The exercise is also made more personal through the use of a dialogue script, one of the dialogue partners being the inner person in one's own dying.

I would urge you to inform the participants in advance of the nature of this exercise. They should know that they will be asked to consider ways that they might die and that they will be carrying on an internal dialogue with themselves about that experience. Explain to them the nature of a dialogue script as a form of writing so that they are prepared for the instruction when it comes during the exercise. Be sure that each person has paper and pen.

Because this exercise is more personal than other exercises of imaging one's own death, some people may feel threatened by it. That feeling should be respected. No pressure should be put on anyone to participate in any of the exercises in this book. I have learned to trust the intuitions of participants concerning the level of their participation. One respondent said of this exercise: "I decided not to participate since the theme was death and bad experiences. The recent murder of a friend of mine is enough to cope with right now." Though the anxiety that this exercise may precipitate is healthy, I would suggest that you do not select this exercise for first-time participants in guided imagery. I say that not because it may be harmful, but because they are likely to gain more benefit from it if they feel more secure about the process of guided imagery. Do not tell participants in advance that they might be threatened by this exercise. This could well induce an anxiety that would otherwise not be there.

### Guided Imagery

Sitting in silence with your eyes closed . . . letting your breathing come more slowly and deeply . . . concentrating on your breathing and its easy and relaxed movement . . . breathing more slowly and deeply . . . letting out a sigh as you exhale . . . breathing in . . . and breathing out . . . breathing in . . . and breathing out . . . feeling your body relax, and your attention moving naturally and easily to the interior of your self . . . quieting your thoughts about activities in the external world . . . letting them fade away . . . focusing your energy inward as you prepare yourself for a dialogue with your innermost self.

In your mind's eye imagine different ways in which you might die. Let the images form spontaneously, trusting that they will be realistic in relation to inner awareness and anticipation. For example, there may be no objective reason that you can give for a deep-seated fear of being stabbed with a knife, but the fear is realistic in the inner world of your awareness. On the other hand, there may be risks that come with your work that will suggest an image of the way in which you may die, or risks that come with the genes you have inherited in a family with a history of cancer or heart disease. As the images form, make a list of from four to six ways in which you might die. **(Pause for 1–2 minutes)**

After you have completed the list of possible ways that you might die, choose from the list the way of dying which generates the most feeling in you. It may not be the most objectively realistic, but choose it anyway if you feel strongly about it and are willing to reflect on it more deeply. When you have made your selection, close your eyes and return to the realm of your inner self. As you focus your attention on this particular way in which you may die, identify some of the things from your past which suggest to you that this may be the way in which you will die. That may take you back prior to the time of your birth as you recall the way that your parents or grandparents died. It may take you back to a near-death experience when you were younger or to a trauma caused by the death of someone you loved very much. There will likely be a whole history of things which lead up to your selection of this particular way in which you may die. Let images rise from your inner awareness without effort on your part. Record those images without concern about sequence or why you should be remembering *that* particular incident which seems to have no particular relevance. Trust your intuitions as you construct a history of your anticipation of this particular way of dying. **(Pause for 4–5 minutes)**

To ready yourself for writing a dialogue script with the event of your dying, close your eyes and return to the realm of your inner awareness. In your mind's eye construct a room deep within the interior of your self. Furnish it in any way that you wish. Make it a place that is comfortable for you, perhaps with a picture window looking out on your favorite kind of scenery. It is a place where you will not be disturbed, where you can relax and be comfortable with yourself. Imagine yourself seated comfortably in this room, letting yourself feel the presence of the inner person within the event of your dying. Let yourself feel the inner continuity of your life: its present, its past, and its movement into the future. Your anticipation of the way that you will die has a personal history that is part of the inner continuity of your life. Your anticipation of what lies ahead can take the form of a person who speaks to you. Feel the presence of the person within this process of anticipating your dying, a person who is a friend and can speak words of wisdom to you. If it feels natural to you, imagine this friend seated in a chair in the inner room of your self, ready to speak with you. Greet that person and say whatever comes to you, whatever you would like to say to the person who is your dying, and let that be the beginning of the dialogue script.

Say whatever you have to say to the inner person of your dying and then listen for the response. The response will come from the inner person of your dying as that has developed within you, and its words will reflect that movement. They may be words of warning about how you are living your life. They may be words of assurance to calm your fears of dying. They may be words of wisdom about the meaning of death and what lies beyond. You are simply to record what is said as it comes, without editing, without directing it, without censoring it. The words flow through your pen to the paper, and so you record the inner dialogue that takes place. It speaks and you speak, and your pen records the words which are spoken. The dialogue continues on its own without direction until all that needs to be said has been said. (**Allow 20–25 minutes for writing**)

## DIALOGUE WITH YOUR BODY ABOUT THE END OF LIFE

*Notes for the Leader*

We can learn a great deal about dying from those who are dying, but we know next to nothing about death because no one has come back from the other side to tell us about it. The one clear certainty in death is the fate of the body. At the time of death all the vital signs of life are gone. The body is still, grows cold and rigid, and soon begins to decay. The reality of death as an end to life is nowhere more clear than in the fate of the body. Most Christians cope with this reality through their belief in the separation of soul and body at the time of death and their confidence that the soul goes directly to God in heaven. Other Christians see the fate of the body to be the fate of the whole person, but take comfort in the promise of the resurrection of the body, which is the resurrection of the whole person. However one may think about the interim between death and resurrection, there is no question about the fate of the body at the time of death.

Since a dialogue with their body will likely be a new and somewhat strange experience for most people, the following two paragraphs are suggestive of the way you might introduce this exercise:

The purpose of a dialogue with the body about the end of life is to enable you to be more realistic about death as an ending. We may be tempted sometimes to use our faith in life after death to deny some of the harsh realities of death, and particularly the harsh reality of what happens to the body. The Christian faith at its best is a resource for facing reality, not denying it. To give that part of yourself which is your body a voice, a voice that can speak to you of its certain demise, is a way of lending reality to your death. Rather than fostering a sense of separation between body and self, this exercise can bring about a stronger sense of identification between the two.

All too often we treat our bodies as our possessions, to use and misuse as we wish. Scripture speaks of the body as an essential part of the self, the whole of which is a gift from God that is sacred and to be treated with deep respect. St. Paul goes so far as to speak of the body as "a temple of the Holy Spirit within you" (1 Cor 6:19). The voice of the body can be a vehicle for the voice of God. That is the purpose of the dialogue which follows.

The idea of the body as a person with a voice will probably not make much sense to people apart from the imagery experience. However, we all share an intuitive sense that the body has a life of its own and certainly a death of its own. When asked to imagine themselves as a corpse, a typical response will be: "That's not me!" In the realm of twilight imagery, the imagination will be able to give the body a voice which can speak to the person who is housed in that body.

Make sure everyone is supplied with paper and pen. Advise the participants that they will be writing both during the exercise and at its close.

### Guided Imagery

Uncross your legs and arms and relax your body as much as you can in the chairs where you are seated . . . letting your eyes close as your body relaxes . . . letting the sound of my voice and the sound of the music guide you ever so gently into the center of yourself . . . attuning yourself to the world within rather than the world without . . . listening to the voice of your body rather than to the voices outside of you that are always demanding your attention . . .

As you settle comfortably into the region of your inner self, be aware of your body from within rather than looking at your body from the outside, as something external to you. Be aware of your body from within, your breathing in and out in a natural, regular rhythm. Be aware of any tensions in your body and let those tensions go so that your body can feel relaxed and at ease. Pay attention to some of the needs of your body, needs that perhaps you have been ignoring because of some of the pressing things which you have to do. In your mind's eye go to those places in your body where you feel some tension or pain and acknowledge the need that is being voiced by your body. . . . Reflect for a moment on the wonders of your body and how smoothly it functions without any effort on your part—your vision, more perfect than the most intricate of cameras . . . your voice and your ears, by which you hear and are heard . . . your body sensations when touching and being touched . . . Breathe a prayer of thanksgiving for the body that is you.

In order to ready yourself for a dialogue with your body about the end of life, you need to become aware of the inner continuity of its life history. In that way you can meet the person within the process of your physical life. To do so while maintaining a focus on the end of life, recall past experiences in your life when your body experienced loss or the threat of loss. List those experiences on the left-hand side of the paper as they occur to you. Do not be concerned about chronological order or the relative importance of the various items. What you list will be related to memories of experiences. It may have been the experience of a serious illness or an accident. It may be the experience of living with a disability through the partial or total loss of some bodily function. It may be the experience of aging, the slow process of bodily disintegration. Open the doors of your memory and let experiences of bodily loss surface in your mind. It is enough to put down a single word or phrase to remind yourself of the total experience. (**Pause for 3–4 minutes**)

After you have completed the list, redo the sequence of items in chronological order on the right side of the paper. Doing so will give you a sense of the continuity of your body life as experiences of loss have impinged on that life. (**Pause for 1 minute**)

You are now ready for a dialogue with your body about the end of life. Sitting in quietness with your eyes closed . . . focusing your attention inward . . . you feel the presence of your body as a person, a person within the process of the life of your body. As you feel the presence of your body as a person grow stronger within you, you may be aware of images forming from within the depths of your inner person. If so, make note of them and record them. Remaining in quietness with your eyes closed, let the presence of your body as a person grow stronger. As you feel ready, greet it as a person and say to your body whatever is on your mind and heart about the end of life, and then listen to how your body responds. Listen closely to what your body has to say about the end of life from its perspective, responding to what has been said only after you have indicated that you fully understand it. In this way the dialogue script is underway. Record both what you say and what the person within your body says. The dialogue will flow on its own. Your pen simply records what is there without censoring or interpreting. Let the inner speaking proceed in silence. **(Allow 20–25 minutes for writing)**

## CARE FOR THE DYING

*Notes for the Leader*
      A guided imagery exercise in the care of the dying can serve two purposes. First, it can help people to prepare themselves for a time when they will need to care for the dying by helping them to identify resources within themselves for that task. Second, it can help people to reflect on how well they will be able to receive care from others at the time of their own dying. The following exercise is designed for both purposes since they are so closely intertwined. As a result, the exercise is longer than most others and maybe too long for some groups or for the time you have allotted for the exercise.
      You may want to consider dividing the exercise into "Care for the Dying" and "Caring for Oneself While Dying." One reason for keeping the exercise as a single unit is that a person who has confronted the reality of his own dying will be much more sensitive, open, and honest in providing care for those who are dying. One way to retain the unity while dividing the exercise is to invite some sharing in between the divided exercise.
      Students preparing themselves for a medical career should find this exercise helpful in anticipating their first assignment in caring for a terminally ill patient and perhaps forestalling a comment that I have heard from more than one terminally ill person: "I felt as though I had to take care of her rather than the other way around." This exercise should also prove helpful to those persons who have elderly parents or grandparents that they will likely care for.
      The exercise calls for participants to choose a person to care for. They are asked to choose someone who has already died. However, you can easily adapt the exercise so that they are directed to provide care for someone who is likely to need their care. It is better not to advise them ahead of time that they will be making this choice. That will rob the

exercise of its spontaneity. It will be enough to tell them that the exercise is designed to assist them in future tasks of caring for the dying.

If at all possible, encourage some sharing of experiences at the close of this exercise, perhaps in small groups or each person talking with a person nearby. If that is not feasible, the leader should say something like the following:

> You may discover through this exercise that it is much easier for you to provide care for the dying than it is for you to receive it. The old adage that it is better to give than to receive is firmly embedded in the Christian consciousness of most of us. But for everybody who gives care there has to be somebody who receives it, and by the law of averages that means that we will be on the receiving end once in a while. Not many of us are prepared for that, however, and we cringe at the thought of becoming dependent. Care-giving and care-receiving go hand in hand; after all, one's "self" is as legitimate an object of care as the self of others.

## Guided Imagery

Sitting in the quiet and calm of this protected space with eyes closed, removed from the noise and busyness of the outside world, uncross your arms and legs, and find a relaxed position for your body . . . becoming aware of your breathing . . . breathing in and breathing out . . . feeling yourself gradually becoming one with your breathing . . . in tune with the breathing that is you . . . adapting yourself to the natural rhythm of your breathing . . . feeling the tensions of the day float away . . . letting your body feel more and more relaxed, tensions draining away like water flowing down the side of a hill.

In the quiet and calm of your inner space, so relaxed that your body feels as though it is floating in air, be aware of the goodness of being alive at this very moment, whatever problems you may have. . . . Feel the peace of being alone with yourself and in touch with the deeper part of yourself, your spiritual self. . . . Feel the unity with others who share your concern for the dying and who want, like you, to provide gentle care for their human spirit as well as their ravaged bodies. . . .

In the quiet and calm of your inner being, so relaxed that your body feels as though it is floating in air, let your mind drift back over the years in an unhurried, leisurely pace and remember people you have known who have died. Let the memories come spontaneously. You may be surprised at some of the names and faces that come to your mind . . . . . As those names and faces come to you, jot them down, opening your eyes just long enough to put the name or the initials on the paper and then returning to the region of your inner self. As you write each name, remember the circumstances around the dying and some of the feelings you had at the time. Take a few moments to complete that list. For some of you it will be short, for others longer. **(Pause 3–5 minutes)**

When you have completed the list, select from among the names you have placed there a person whose dying was gradual rather than sudden, preferably a person with whom you spent some time while he or she was dying. It doesn't have to be the most important person on the list, not even someone that you knew well. If you have had no occasion to be with a person who was dying, imagine being with a person on your list whom you wish that you could have been with while he or she was dying. **(Pause for 30 seconds)**

With your eyes closed, feeling safe in the quiet and calm of this protected space, enter or reenter the experience of being with someone who is dying for whom you have a deep, caring attitude. Picture that person in your mind at different stages of your knowing him or her: first during a time of relatively good health . . . then at the onset of the illness . . . and then at different stages of the process of dying. . . . Be aware of your reaction to the growing awareness of the imminence of his or her dying . . . As you let that awareness deepen in your heart and mind, focus on your relationship to the person at the end-stage of his or her dying. Imagine yourself being at your present age even if you were much younger when the death occurred.

Picture in your mind's eye the place where you and the person are located. You can choose any location you wish and furnish it in a manner that makes it a good place for both of you to be, a place where you would feel comfortable either in giving or in receiving care. Let that scene come clearly in your mind and let yourself blend slowly into that scene . . . In your mind's eye, approach the bedside and look into the eyes of the person who is dying. What do you see there? What are you feeling as you gaze into the eyes of this person who is coming close to the end of his or her life? What is the hardest thing for you about being there? Is it a sense of personal loss? or a feeling of inadequacy? or a fear of your own dying? What needs are you aware of in the person who is dying? Though you will be aware of both physical and emotional needs, focus on the spiritual needs, the needs of the human spirit. What is it that the person most needs from you? Is it some form of assurance that you are there and that God is there? Is it a reminder of God's forgiveness that is needed? Is it reassurance that everything will be O.K.?

How adequate do you feel in meeting those needs? How ready would you be to pray for or with this person? Imagine yourself asking if he or she would like you to offer a prayer. What reaction do you see in his or her face? What is it you feel within yourself? As you are ready, write down some of the feelings and thoughts which come from within the experience of caring for someone who is dying. Let the writing flow spontaneously without analysis or criticism from the rational side of your brain. **(Allow 15–20 minutes for writing)**

Closing your eyes once again, and feeling safe in the calm and quiet of your inner world, return to the room where you were before, only this time imagine yourself as the one who is dying and being cared for by anyone that you would like to select for that role. Choose someone with whom you would be comfortable. It can be someone who is no longer alive or even someone who doesn't know you but whom you know and respect. **(Pause for 1 minute)**

Picture your ravaged body close to the time of your death. Imagine yourself lying in bed, looking into the eyes of the person who is caring for you. What do you see there? What are you feeling as you gaze into the eyes of this person who is there to meet your needs? What is the hardest thing for you in being cared for? Is it fear of facing the reality of your dying? Is it fear of rejection, fear of being abandoned? Is it hard for you to admit your need of others, hard to ask for what you need? What needs are you aware of in yourself? Though there will be physical and emotional needs, focus on the spiritual needs. Do you have confidence that the person taking care of you could meet those needs if you could ask for the help you need? Would you like this person to pray for or with you? Imagine yourself asking him or her to offer a prayer. What is it you feel as you ask and what answer do you expect? What reaction do you see in his or her face?

Take a moment to let the experience deepen, and then as you are ready, write down some of the feelings and thoughts which come from within the experience of being cared for in your dying. Let the writing flow spontaneously without analysis or criticism from the rational side of your brain. **(Allow 10–15 minutes for writing)**

# 9. In Anticipation of Grieving

The purpose of the exercises in Chapter 8 was to aid individuals to anticipate their dying. That is a form of grieving, anticipatory grieving over the losses which are inevitable in the process of dying, including the loss of control, life's purpose and meaning, goals for the future, and significant relationships. The exercises in this chapter deal with grieving over the losses sustained through death, including one's own death. Since such grieving for Christians always takes place within the context of the resurrection, there are two exercises which focus on images of hope.

## MY FUNERAL

*Notes for the Leader*

Many people have described spontaneous fantasies of being present at their funeral service. One need that is satisfied through such fantasies is the need for recognition. There is curiosity about who will come, what they will say, how many flowers will be sent and by whom, etc. It may also be that such a fantasy satisfies the need for a sense of immortality. After all, I can't really be dead if I can observe what's going on at my funeral. It is not the purpose of this exercise to meet either of those needs, but rather to provide a perspective on life that is possible only after it has ended and to gain a sense of the funeral liturgy as "passage" through death to life. It has often been said, also by me, that funerals are for the living, not the dead. This exercise is no exception to that rule in that the person who imagines her funeral *is* living. Experiencing one's own funeral can be an occasion for reflecting on one's earthly life and its struggle for fulfillment in partial and ambiguous ways while at the same time celebrating the passage from life to Life with its completion of being.

Some might wonder whether the experience of being present at one's own funeral, including the viewing of one's own body, might not evoke strong feelings of anxiety or sadness. Though some participants do report feelings of fear and sadness, I was surprised that a large majority of them report either no emotion or peaceful feelings. If there is sadness, it is mostly the sadness that others feel.

Almost all of the participants reported that the liturgical experience of transformation from darkness and death to light and life was realistic and full of meaning. As one person put it, "It helped me complete my journey. The experience was very satisfying in that I finally knew where my soul-body went."

Advise the participants that they will be doing some writing both during and at the close of the exercise. Be sure that everyone is supplied with pen and paper.

### Guided Imagery

Let your eyes close to keep distractions away from the inner world that you are about to enter. Shutting out the noise and the distractions of the outside world, you seek in this place a time for stillness and peace . . . letting your body relax and your mind float free . . . ridding yourself of all the thoughts that crowd into your consciousness . . . letting them fly away like birds freed from a cage . . . letting the stillness fill your being as all distractions of sight and hearing fade away . . . hearing only the sound of my voice as you go deeper and deeper into the solitude of your inner being, there to create a room for yourself apart from the noise and distractions of a busy and sometimes stressful life. Furnish the room in any way that you like. It is for you and you alone, a place where you can be free from the demands of others and alone with the thoughts and feelings of your inner self. Make it a room that invites reflection, perhaps with a scenic view from a picture window. Resting comfortably on a reclining chair, breathing becomes easy and steady. Stillness deepens in the room and in yourself.

Imagine that you have been given a special dispensation to be present at your own funeral. Let an image form in your mind of where it will take place. It should be a church, but can be any church you choose—the church where you now worship, another church that has special meaning for you, or a church that you construct with the aid of your imagination. Picture in your mind some of the people that you would like to be there, including, if you wish, persons who have already died.

Let an image of a casket form in your mind, a casket in which you have been placed. Over a portion of the casket is a white cloth, a baptismal pall that serves as a reminder of your Christian identity as one who has died and risen with Christ. Directly behind the casket stands a cross with a life-size figure of Christ on it, not slumped over in a posture of death and defeat, but with arms outstretched in victory and wearing the crown of a king.

Let the image of that cross and the image of your casket blend into one image so that the outstretched arms of the victorious Christ enfold and lift up the casket. Experience the life-giving power that envelops the casket. Feel the reassurance of being in the caring presence of that life-giving power.

Before the funeral begins, there is a last viewing of the body, your body. Picture that scene in your mind as if you were an unseen observer. Who are some of the people you see there? What kind of expression do you see on their faces as they file by the casket? What are some of the things that they are saying and thinking as they go by? **(Pause for 1–2 minutes)** From the position of an unseen observer, imagine yourself viewing your own body in the casket. Are you surprised at what you see and feel? How have you been dressed? How old were you at the time of your death? Express in writing some of your thoughts and feelings as you reflect on seeing others and yourself viewing your body. **(Allow 5–10 minutes for writing)**

In your mind's eye, imagine yourself as an unseen observer of your funeral service. The day is dark and overcast with the threat of rain. The weather outside mirrors the mood inside the building. At the beginning of the liturgy the church is darkened except for four candles positioned at the four corners of your casket, but as the liturgy unfolds the church brightens until at the end sunlight is bursting through every window and your casket is bathed in light. As the liturgy concludes, imagine everything in that scene fading away except the casket—people, pastor, church—until all that is left is your casket bathed in bright light, light that appears even brighter in its being reflected by the white baptismal pall. The light intensifies until the casket bursts into bright flames which consume the casket until it is reduced to ashes, and then imagine yourself emerging, phoenix-like, out of the ashes, wrapped in the shining cloak of your baptismal pall. Imagine yourself as whole and well, free from all imperfections and no longer tainted by sin; you are the person you've always hoped you might be. As you emerge from the ashes perfectly whole, you are met by an angel or a being of light who is as familiar to you as you are to yourself. And you are aware that you have passed from darkness to light, from death to life, and yet you are surprised at how familiar you are to your surroundings. What brought gladness to your heart before is here in even fuller measure, but what brought sadness and pain is present no longer and faded in memory. You are aware that you have moved to a different dimension of time and space beyond the gates of death.

As you feel ready, let your pen express the feelings and thoughts of your inner self as you reflect on your funeral as a passage from death to life, made real and concrete in the death and resurrection of Christ, his Passover and yours collapsed into a single event in your funeral liturgy. **(Allow 15–20 minutes for writing)**

## REFLECTIONS ON A FUNERAL

*Notes for the Leader*

This exercise is designed to help people reflect on funerals which they have attended in the past and to focus on one experience in particular. It will be especially helpful for those who have not completed their grieving over past deaths. As part of your introductory remarks, you might explain that grieving which is not completed at the time of the loss will remain as a task to be completed at another time. Some people may be surprised at how strong their feelings are as they recall the experience of a funeral which they thought was a thing of the past. This is also a useful exercise in death education. Funerals are the only public events in which death is recognized as the formal end of life. Since almost everybody has attended at least one funeral by the age of ten, it provides an opportunity for reflecting on the coping skills which they and others have used when responding to the death of a loved one.

### *Guided Imagery*

As you let your eyes close and your body relax, feel the tug of the interior life draw you deeper and deeper into yourself . . . letting your breathing become steady and slow . . . letting the stillness fill your inner being with peace . . . feeling the goodness of being alive and able to

breathe without effort . . . breathing in . . . and breathing out . . .
breathing in . . . and breathing out . . . concentrating on your breathing
. . . letting its rhythm be the tempo of your inner self . . . letting the
thoughts and concerns of your life settle like sediment to the bottom of
your mind . . . leaving the waters of your life clear and calm.

As you sit quietly in the protected calm of your interior world, let
your thoughts drift back over the years and recall the memories of funerals which have made a personal impact on you. There may have been
many such experiences or only a few, depending on the age and circumstances of your life. Choose no more than six funerals that you have attended, jotting them down as you recall them. Perhaps it will be a funeral
of someone very close to you—a parent, a spouse, a child, a friend. Perhaps it will be a very early memory of a funeral which gave you a deep
impression of the power and mystery of death. Perhaps it will be a funeral where you were impressed by someone who gave a powerful witness to the meaning of faith. I will give you a moment to spontaneously
recall up to six funerals that you can remember. They don't need to be
in chronological order. Let your selections be made spontaneously from
within the interior of your self rather than choosing those funerals which
you think should be important. **(Pause for 2–3 minutes)**

Looking over the choices you have made, select one from among
them which evokes the strongest feelings, which seems to be the most
significant for you at this particular time, realizing that your choice
might be different next week or next year. With the aid of your memory
and the power of your imagination, reenter that experience. Try to form
an image in your mind of the person that you were then. How old were
you? What was your relationship to the person who died, and how did
his or her death affect you? Recall your feelings as you remember the
location of the funeral, the liturgy that was used, the casket, and the final
committal. **(Pause for 2–3 minutes)** What were your needs at that time,
especially your spiritual needs, and how were they met by those who
were with you at the funeral? Was there one person who was especially
helpful and what did he or she do? How well aware were you of what
was happening and what you were feeling? Were you on the giving or
the receiving end of comfort and reassurance? Or perhaps both? What
happened to your faith in this experience? Was it weakened or strength-
ened by this encounter with death? What or who was most helpful to you

in your struggle of faith at that time? What was it that you learned from that experience which has made a difference in your life since that time? As you feel ready, express the feelings and thoughts which emerge from within the experience of this funeral by writing freely and spontaneously whatever emerges from the experience. For example, you may feel anger at being abandoned by a person on whom you were very dependent. Don't question the feeling. Simply express what you feel with whatever words that seem appropriate. The writing is a way of integrating the experience more fully into the totality of your life. **(Allow 15–20 minutes for writing)**

## GRIEVING THE LOSS OF ANOTHER

*Notes for the Leader*
This is an exercise in anticipatory grief. The purpose of the previous exercise was to help people complete the grieving which they have yet to do in relation to a previous loss. The purpose of the following exercise is to help people prepare for losses yet to come. Those who are close to someone who is terminally ill do that naturally as a way of coping with a loss that they know is inevitable; the more of that they do prior to the death, the less they will need to do later. It is not necessary, however, for a person to be terminally ill before one can anticipate his loss. Though it would not be healthy to dwell on that loss all of the time, it can be helpful on occasion to imagine a world in which that person was no longer present. This exercise will guide the imagination in such an experience.

Participants report that this exercise is harder for them to do than one in which they anticipate their own death. They find it difficult to choose the person whom they will mourn. One person thought it cruel to choose and another considered it to be a bad omen, both feeling at an unconscious level that this exercise would cause what they imagine to actually happen. The funeral service seems both unreal and far too real. The most resistance came at the burial site, and especially in response to the suggestion that dirt be thrown on the coffin. One person said: "I could not even imagine throwing dirt on the casket. It was a very strong restraining force and very strange." Another said that this was "not quite real because I was too afraid to let it seem real or imagine it too deeply.'' Still another: ''It really scared me to think that I would have to do this someday.'' Despite the resistance, there was no evidence that any of the participants failed to maintain control of their experience.

Since it is difficult to do, it may be tempting to eliminate that portion of the exercise where participants throw dirt on the casket at the burial site. That would not be wise since this act signals the final ending. Participants may not be able to fully experience this event, but they should be given the opportunity to experience as much of it as they can.

The fact that participants find this exercise more difficult than imagining their own death is not surprising. The dying must cope with endings, but the survivor must not only endure the ending, but also the wilderness wandering and often painful process of new beginning. The same is true for those who do anticipatory grieving.

It will be necessary to make some adjustments in the funeral portion of this exercise if those engaging in the exercise have no experience with traditional funeral liturgies.


### *Guided Imagery*

Let the tension flow from your body as you relax comfortably in the chair on which you are sitting, letting it bear the weight of your body . . . As you sit in silence with your eyes closed, your breathing comes regularly and slowly without effort and without thought. Imagine yourself lying in lush grass by the side of a small stream on a warm and sunny day. It is easy and natural to rest in the quiet of that tranquil place, hearing only the sounds of the wind rustling through the leaves of trees and water gently flowing through a rippling brook. Let the breathing come slowly and evenly in the calm of that place, in the calm of your inner self.

In the calm and tranquil peace of your inner self, choose some member of your immediate family whose death you will likely mourn sometime in the future. Choose a member of the family with whom you have some regular interaction and whose death would be experienced as a significant loss to you. You may want to choose someone very close to you, like husband or wife, as a way of preparing yourself for what might happen. Or you may want to choose someone, like parent or grandparent, whose death is likely to come sooner than for other members of your family because of age or illness. I will give you a moment to make that choice. Let yourself spontaneously choose who this might be by trusting your intuitions and your own felt sense about whose death you feel ready to experience and reflect upon. **(Pause for 1–2 minutes)**

With the aid of your imagination picture the scene where you will talk for the last time with the person who is dying. Choose an appropriate place for this conversation, a place where you can feel relaxed and comfortable. It may be the home of the person whom you have chosen or a place where both of you have been that is treasured by you. Imagine yourself in conversation with this person for what you know will be the last time. Let the image of that person's face come clearly into your mind. What is it that you would like to say, knowing that these will be the last words that you will ever speak to him or her? With the image of this person's face firmly fixed in your mind, imagine yourself looking deeply into his or her eyes and expressing what is in your mind and heart. **(Pause for 1–2 minutes)** Now listen carefully to what he or she has to say to you in return. Let a conversation flow back and forth as you let the drama of this moment unfold. **(Pause for 3–4 minutes)**

Now imagine yourself at the funeral service after this person has died. Picture the casket in front of the altar of a church. The casket is open prior to the service, and you along with others file past for one last moment of farewell. Imagine yourself passing in front of the casket for just a moment. The casket is then closed, and a baptismal pall is placed over it as a reminder that this person has already died the death of sin and risen to new life through his or her baptism. Who are some of the people that you would want to be there? What kind of worship service would you want it to be? Would you want those attending to participate or only silently observe? What hymns, if any, would you wish to be sung? What Scripture readings would provide the most comfort to you? During the service you are asked to say a few words about the person who has died, what he or she has meant to you and why you think that he or she will live on in memory. What would you want to say on such an occasion? As you imagine yourself sitting through the funeral liturgy, what is the hardest part of that experience? What is the most comforting? Let your thoughts and feelings be transmitted through the pen to the paper in front of you as you reflect on the meaning of this ritual parting. **(Allow 10–15 minutes for writing)**

Imagine yourself now at the place of burial. Picture an open grave with the casket suspended on straps above it, ready to be lowered into the ground. Observe the people who are there, gathered around the grave for a final farewell. Hear the words of the pastor or priest commending the body to the earth from which it came with an affirmation of the promise of the resurrection. At the conclusion of the service watch the casket being lowered slowly into the grave. Imagine yourself taking a spade and shoveling some fresh dirt into the hole and onto the casket as a way of experiencing the finality of the separation. Now let yourself feel the comforting presence of those around you (family, friends, congregation members) who share both the experience of the loss and the faith which sustains you in the experience of loss. **(Pause for 2–3 minutes)**

With the aid of your imagination, join your whole extended family at your home or at the home of some other member of the family immediately following the committal service. If your family has been close, let yourself experience the goodness of that fellowship, the exchange of embraces, the sharing of memories, the laughter at the good times and the tears at the sad times. Feel the solidity and support of those family relationships. If you came from a family with strained relationships, imagine this family gathering as a time of reconciliation and healing. Reflect for a moment on the meaning of family relationships. Let an image of each member of your family form in your mind. What, if anything, do you want to change in your relationship to each of them as you reflect on the fragility of life? **(Pause for 2–3 minutes)**

Finally, in your mind's eye picture yourself six months following the funeral service. Try to imagine what life would be like without this person as part of your life. What would be the hardest adjustment for you to make? What kinds of needs would have gone unmet because of the absence of this special person? How do you think those needs would be met now? Who is the person to whom you would turn most readily to talk about your grief? What would you need from that person? What would be the greatest challenge for you as you think about the future, and how would you meet that challenge?

As you feel ready, write for a few moments on your relationship to the person whose death you imagined, beginning with the words: "The way I would like my relationship to . . . to change in the future is . . . ." **(Allow 15–20 minutes for writing)**

## DIALOGUE WITH A PERSON WHO HAS DIED

*Notes for the Leader*

"Grieving the Loss of Another" was an exercise in anticipatory grief, anticipating the loss of someone who is close to you by imagining his or her death and what life would be like without that special person. This exercise is designed to facilitate a dialogue with someone who has died. You might say something like the following to introduce the exercise:

> Relationships don't end with the death of one party, as anyone recently bereaved will tell you. There are so many things that one wishes to share with the other, so many thoughts that lead in the same direction. The relationship is kept alive by the embedded presence of the person who has died in your memory, in your imagination, in your behavior, in the way that you think about yourself as a person. A dialogue with a person who has died can be helpful for a number of different reasons. There may be some unfinished business with this person, things you wish that you had said or done before the person died. There may be something going on in your life right now that you would like to share or for which you need some counsel.
>
> Dialogue with a person who is embedded in your memory and in your imagination is obviously different from face-to-face dialogue with that person. The physical presence of the other person makes the line of differentiation between you and that person clear, though often that line gets fuzzy through mechanisms like projection and identification. A dialogue exercise creates a similar kind of differentiation between you and the other person. An advantage to this exercise over an actual meeting with the person is that you can decide on the appearance and the age of the person as well as the place of meeting. The sense of reality can be very strong if you give yourself fully and freely to this exercise.

Let the participants know that they will be doing some writing during the exercise. Suggest to them the importance of remaining in the experiential mode of inner reflection when they write or make notations. Writing is of fundamental importance in this exercise, and the writing needs to be expressive of the imaginal realm rather than being descriptive or analytic.

## *Guided Imagery*

Sitting in silence, let your eyes close naturally and your breathing come slowly . . . letting the quiet deepen within you as you enter the interior regions of your self . . . becoming aware of your breathing and its natural rhythm . . . breathing in . . . and breathing out . . . breathing in the renewed energy of the life-giving Spirit of God . . . breathing out the tensions in your body and all that weighs you down . . . breathing in the life-giving Spirit of God . . . breathing out the tensions and the tiredness . . . letting your body relax as you adjust yourself to the rhythm of your breathing . . . letting your spirit come alive as you enter the realm of your interior self . . . feeling the peace and the harmony that comes with the relaxation of your body . . . feeling the goodness of being in harmony with yourself, the interior of your self.

In the quietness of this place and in the security of your inner being, recall the names and faces of people you have known who have died. They may be members of your family or good friends, people with whom you were close. You may also include people whom you did not know but who have made a profound impression on you by what they have written or done, people who are wisdom figures or heroes of faith, people who lived long ago but with whom you have developed a strong relationship. As those names and faces begin to surface, write down six or eight names on the paper in front of you, opening your eyes just enough to jot down the name. There may be many names that come to you; select six or eight names which generate the most interest and energy in you. **(Pause for 2–3 minutes)**

After you have completed your list, look over the names and select one person with whom you would like to carry on a dialogue. Of all the people on that list, who is the one person whom you would choose to be with right now? **(Pause for 30 seconds)**

When you have decided on the person with whom you will conduct your dialogue, begin by sitting in silence and preparing yourself in quiet readiness for the inner dialogue you will have with this person. Write down the name of the person at the top of the page, along with the date of your writing. It may be meaningful at a later time. Let a picture of that person form in your mind, allowing yourself spontaneously to choose the appearance and age of that person. As you reflect on your relationship to this person as of this very moment, write a brief paragraph describing the essence of that relationship right now. Don't try to go back to who you were at an earlier time, and don't be too deliberate about what you say. It should include what is negative as well as what is positive in the relationship. Describe the relationship as it is for you right now without making an evaluation of it. **(Pause for 3–4 minutes)**

When you have completed the statement of your present relationship to the person with whom you wish to have a dialogue, settle back into silence. Close your eyes and concentrate on your breathing . . . letting the breath come slowly and softly . . . feeling its natural and regular rhythm . . . concentrating your attention on the person about whom you have written . . . letting images and sounds and physical feelings come to the level of your consciousness . . . letting your mind be flooded with images of special moments in that relationship, sounds or words that you associate with this person, and feelings that are evoked by this special person. **(Pause for 30 seconds)**

Take a few moments in the inner realm of your deeper consciousness, a realm that knows no boundaries of time and space, to let the images and sounds and feelings come of their own accord. Other than keeping the focus on the person you have chosen for a dialogue, make no attempt to guide the experience in a particular direction. The movement takes place of its own accord, and you observe and record the process. Let yourself feel the presence of the other person sharing the space within the inner world of your experience. **(Pause for 2–3 minutes)**

As you sit in silence, feeling the closeness of the other person, let the dialogue proceed. Extend whatever greeting seems appropriate to you. Say what is in your heart to this person. It may be something that was prompted by what you have written or experienced so far, or it may be something altogether different which you are prompted to say or ask. As you write, be aware of the other person who is with you, as close to you as you are to yourself. As you do so, he or she will speak to you. You may hear the voice speaking with its own unique tone and accent, or the speaking may come via your pen. However it happens, let what you say and what is said to you be written in the form of a dialogue script in which you are both speaker and listener.

As you proceed, the dialogue writes itself. At times you may be conscious of what you write and at other times completely caught up in the flow of the dialogue, simply letting your pen record what is being said. The dialogue happens within you. It is not something you create or control. Let it move along any path it wishes to go. You may be surprised at some of the things you talk about and some of the things which are said to you. Simply let that happen, even when what is said by you or the other person doesn't make much sense. Be sure that what you write is the dialogue itself and not a commentary about the dialogue. Later you can reflect on the dialogue and add to it. For now it is important to simply allow the dialogue to take place. **(Allow 20–30 minutes for writing)**

## A JOURNEY BEYOND THE GATES OF DEATH

*Notes for the Leader*

Memory and anticipation are two uniquely human capacities. Anticipation of future fulfillment does not end as one approaches death. Robert Lifton speaks of the need for a sense of historical continuity and describes five different modes of symbolic immortality by which that need is met as human beings face the terminal point of their human existence in this world. One of those modes is religious, and for most Christians it takes the form of anticipation of a heavenly life. In one sense, we are already living on the other side of death because baptism is a participation in Christ's paschal journey through cross to resurrection. Thus we can anticipate the fulfillment of a life that is already deeply rooted in the life of Christ.

The purpose of this exercise is twofold. Experiencing death as passage rather than simply as an end is the first purpose. Belief that death is a gateway to something beyond is not the same thing as experiencing that transition. The second purpose of the exercise is to help participants feel and think positively about death. Death denial is so strong because our imagery of death is so negative. This exercise provides a balance to some of that negativity.

Too often the promise that each of our unique lives will be fulfilled and brought to completion in the age to come is no more than an abstraction. It is a future without empirical definition. We depend on our senses to discern what is real, and since nobody we know has come back from heaven to describe it to us, we have little to feed our imagination. However, descriptions of places where we have never been are accessible to us if those descriptions fit the kind of world with which we are familiar. Images of floating on clouds and playing on harps are not appealing to most of us because they provide no sense of historical continuity between life as we know it and life as we anticipate it in heaven. Guided imagery is a useful tool for establishing a more realistic sense of continuity. The following exercise is designed to help people anticipate the fulfillment of their individual lives in concrete and realistic ways. A portion of the exercise is based on imagery suggested by Ladislas Boros in *Pain and Providence*.

My recommendation is that you tell participants in advance that they will be experiencing a passage through death and into heaven. Do not say anything more than that for fear of detracting from the spontaneity of the imagery formation.

### Guided Imagery

Close your eyes and let your vision turn inward, inward to the center of your being . . . letting your breathing help you to become attuned to your inner rhythm of being . . . feeling all of the tension in your body flowing down and out of you like rain water flowing gently from a roof . . . letting all of your personal concerns and preoccupations fly away like birds freed from a cage . . . letting the sound of the music and my voice guide you inward . . . moving deeper and deeper into the center of yourself . . . listening to the sounds of silence as you experience the peace of being at home with yourself.

In your mind's eye, enter the stream of your life at its beginning and let it carry you forward. You are in a small boat, floating down the stream of your life on a warm summer day . . . past scenes that remind you of significant events in your youth. Most of the time the water flows steadily and evenly down the stream of your life, but at times it becomes turbulent and flows through rocky and twisting channels. As you float down the stream of your life, be aware of both the smooth and the rough portions, both the changes and the continuities, the things which make you afraid and the things which bring gladness to your heart. Feel the goodness of being alive and able to experience the flow of your life, no matter how threatening some portions may be. Feel the excitement, and perhaps anxiety, in anticipating what is beyond the next bend in the stream of your life. **(Pause for 3–4 minutes)**

As you float down the stream of your life, imagine coming to a point where you see a path along the shore, and a sign at the head of the path which reads, "The Place of Your Dying." Docking the boat along the shore, you follow the path which takes you to the place of your dying. Though you may be young, and death may seem part of the distant future, imagine this to be an experience which feels appropriate to the now in your stream of life. Picture the place to which the path leads, the place of your dying. Imagine it in any way you wish it to be—perhaps as a beautiful home in which there is a room set aside for you, furnished in a way that seems good to you. You may choose anyone you wish to be with you. I will give you a few moments to enter fully into that experience with the aid of your imagination. **(Pause for 2–3 minutes)**

Let yourself feel the weariness, the utter exhaustion of your body, as you approach the end of your life. Imagine what it is like to know with certainty that you will die very soon. Feel yourself becoming more and more detached from your surroundings, from those who surround you, from your own body. As you feel yourself drifting away from all that you were attached to in this world, it is as if you had entered a dream world full of mystery and enchantment, though it may be more like going into another world than your usual dreams. Feeling very light, you are aware of drifting out of the bed where your body lies and looking down on it. The experience is strange because you are still conscious of yourself as a whole person. Discovering an open door at the back of the room, you pass through it and stand at the top of ancient stone steps. In the dim light you go down the staircase, not afraid, approaching once again the stream of your life, whose dark waters are now as black as ink. Entering the small boat that you were in before, you float away in the blackness, rocking gently on the water until you pass through a cavernous opening and into warm sunlight. An inner peace and warm glow gradually fill your inner being. You drift on and on. Along the bank the birds are singing and there is freshly cut grass. The people you meet along the way are warm and friendly. They wave you to shore, and you eagerly join them.

It is as if you were waking up on the day you had been looking forward to for a long, long time. There is a keenness in the seeing and hearing of everything around you. It is as if you could see more deeply into the inner core of everything that surrounds you. You feel yourself a part of the rhythm of nature, and you resonate deeply to everything happening around you. You are struck by the genuine warmth and caring of those you meet, and you feel the deeply entrenched defensiveness of the past simply melting away.

Gradually you become aware of how much at home you feel. It's as though all of your life was a journey to this place and this time, and you've finally arrived. All tiredness vanishes, and a sense of contentment and peace takes its place. As you settle into the goodness of being at home, you realize that you are at home with God, and the security you feel is the security that you first felt in the warm embrace and the powerful protection of your mother and father. Here there is unbounded love, love that is not different from what you have experienced before, but fuller, deeper, unconditional, always there, undemanding.

As you relax and give yourself completely to that love, you reflect on the hazards of your journey and the wonder of having arrived safely at this place of complete joy and fulfillment. With a heart filled with peace, you grasp fully for the first time that death has led you to the peaking of life, to its richest fulfillment, to its mysterious depths. As you reflect on the meaning of death and the heavenly life which lies beyond it, begin to write some of the thoughts and feelings which spontaneously surface in your consciousness. **(Allow 15–20 minutes for writing)**

## AN IMAGE OF HOPE

*Notes for the Leader*

This brief exercise is based on an actual experience of Brother Lawrence, a seventeenth-century Carmelite whose sayings have helped many to a better understanding of mystical experience. Its purpose is to help people experience hope in the center of despair, life in the center of death, resurrection at the center of the cross.

If there is time and the nature of the group allows it, encourage individuals to share what they have written.

## *Guided Imagery*

Sitting in the quietness of this protected place, with eyes closed and breathing even, the self within grows quiet. Thoughts that have been darting in and out of the mind diminish in intensity and gradually ebb away. It is quiet now as you move toward the interior of your self. Centered and still within your inner self, only the breath is moving . . . moving in . . . and moving out of the center of your self. It is quiet at the center of your self, and peaceful.

Select from the storehouse of your memory a time when you felt particularly desolate and without hope. Perhaps it was a time when you were feeling particularly bad about yourself, a time when nothing was going right, a time of failure and feeling inadequate. Perhaps it was a time when you lost someone on whom you were very dependent and saw no way that you could manage a future without him or her. Whatever the circumstances were, experience now what you were feeling then of despair, hopelessness, and helplessness. **(Pause for 2-3 minutes)**

In your mind's eye imagine yourself walking through a wooded area on a cold and wet November day in Maine. The sky is overcast. A drizzle is falling. You are all alone. As you look around you, you are struck by the bleakness of everything you see. Everything is gray and dark. The trees and the shrubs are bare. There is no sign of life anywhere. The wind is cold and damp, penetrating to the marrow of your bones. The whole world is a mirror of the desolation within your soul: bleak, barren, and lifeless. **(Pause for 1–2 minutes)**

As you trudge slowly through the woods on a path that leads nowhere, you find yourself reflecting on the ebb and flow of life. These barren trees which seem so lifeless will once again be covered with leaves which will rustle gently in the summer sun. This dark and dreary forest will again teem with life of all kinds: lush vegetation on the forest floor, the sound of birds from every tree, the sun filtering through the overhanging branches. How can that be? Only because God gives warmth and light from the sun. Only because God breathed life into a planet that was lifeless and full of chaos. Only because God creates life anew all of the time. Only because God sets our feet upon a path which leads somewhere. **(Pause for 1–2 minutes)**

Imagine in your mind's eye a break in the thick cloud cover of that overcast day and the sun shining through. Imagine that bleak winter sun gaining strength until you can feel the rays from that sun beaming warmer and warmer until it has the intensity of a summer sun. Imagine that the woods through which you walk are slowly transformed from November to May, from a dreary overcast day to a bright and sunny one, from barren lifelessness all around you to a forest covered with green and filled with spring flowers. Feel the surge of life around you and within you. Feel the goodness of being alive at this very moment, no matter how many storms are on the horizon. Feel the blessing of God upon you and everything that lives. **(Pause for 2–3 minutes)**

As you feel ready, reflect on this experience and ones similar to it in your life when you have discovered hope in the midst of despair, life in the midst of death. What has helped you to find hope when there seemed to be none? As you feel ready, write for a few moments from within an experience of hopelessness and helplessness. Let your pen record what it is that you draw on in such moments to sustain and enliven you. **(Allow 15–20 minutes for writing)**

# 10. In Anticipation of Loss

The exercises in this chapter are more varied and less focused than those in Chapters 8 and 9. The general theme has to do with endings in life, the assumption being that all of life is filled with loss and that all of these losses are mini-deaths that can help us to prepare for the way that we deal with the permanent losses we face in the death of others and ourselves.

## ENDINGS

*Notes for the Leader*

Most of our attention in this book has been focused on death, the end of life. Our life, however, is full of endings, each of which shares some of the quality of the final ending. Some of the endings are an inevitable part of normal human development, such as leaving home and retirement. Other endings are situational and often tragic, such as divorce or losing a job. Every loss in life is a death equivalent to a greater or lesser degree.

Each transition in life calls for an ending, though the ending is usually ignored. The attention is focused on the new beginning. Take graduation as an example. I've attended commencement exercises at the university where I teach for over twenty years. The challenge of the future is the consistent theme of the addresses at these events. Nobody talks about the endings: the loss of a community that nurtured the student's identity through crucial years of development, the loss of beloved mentors, the loss of treasured friendships. The same can be said for other transitions like marriage. Little attention is given to the deeply symbolic ritual of "*leaving* father and mother" as one is joined to a husband or wife. We treat the endings in the midst of life much the same as we do the endings at the close of life. We ignore them.

Explain the purpose of this exercise before beginning the guided imagery. There are references to endings already in the induction, and participants will more readily enter into the experience if they are prepared in advance to reflect on endings. Be sure that participants are equipped with pen and paper for the writing portion of the exercise. Tell them in advance that they will be doing some writing during as well as at the end of the exercise. Encourage them to stay within the experiential mode of the exercise when they are writing, keeping their vision focused on their inner experience at all times.

To introduce this exercise to participants, you might say something like the following:

> This exercise is designed to help you reflect on the endings in your life. You can learn a great deal about how you will cope with the end of life by reflecting on the way that you cope with endings during your life. Your style of coping is not likely to change. If you have a hard time saying goodbye to others, then the loss of the other in death will probably be hard for you. If you are plagued with guilt feelings much of the time, then fear of judgment is likely to be prominent in your fear of dying. If you are cautious about taking chances with the future, then the fear of the unknown in death will be hard for you to cope with. Thus a time of reflection on endings in life can help you to identify what may be difficult for you in the losses you experience through death and to find better ways to cope with those losses.

At the end of the exercise it might be helpful to say something like the following:

> What you may have discovered through this exercise is that you have developed a particular style of dealing with endings in your life. If you had trouble getting in touch with memories of endings in your life, might that not suggest a pattern of avoidance? It may be that your style of coping is rational control, or perhaps this exercise triggered feelings of anxiety that you wished to ward off. Each of us has a different way of coping. It's important for you to distinguish your way of coping with endings from that of others so that you do not impose your way on others. You may also begin to recognize the limitations of your way of coping and search for alternative ways to cope.

### Guided Imagery

Let your body relax and your mind become still. Close your eyes so that you see what is within you, deep within the center of your self

. . . letting the silence still your soul . . . letting your breathing become slower and easier . . . feeling the natural rhythm of the movement of your breathing in and out . . . moving within the rhythm of your breathing to the center of your self . . . exploring the memories of your life, a life full of beginnings and endings . . . entering the quiet waters of the stream of your life . . . flowing slowly past scenes that evoke memories of beginning and endings . . . letting the waters of the stream of your life carry you along, through turbulent, swiftmoving waters in narrow passages, and through gently moving currents in broad, even spaces . . . reflecting on your life . . . beginnings and endings . . . changing currents . . . breathing easily and naturally in the silence . . . looking inward to the center of the self . . . entering quietly into the stream of your life at the very beginning of its origin.

As you gently float down the waters that form the stream of your life, recall the earliest experiences of endings that you can remember. The earliest memories may be no more than a feeling of apprehension at the thought of separation from your mother or some other trusted adult. It may have been an ending which brought chaos into your life, like a death in the family. Or it may have been a happy ending, like not having to wear a cast on an arm or leg that you broke. You may have memories of endings which were insignificant to everyone but you, like your parents' departure on a trip without you, or the death of a pet, or a friend moving away. Note five or six such experiences of ending prior to the age of twelve in any order that they come to you. Stay within the experience of floating down the stream of your life, opening your eyes just long enough to jot down a word or phrase that is associated with the ending you are recalling. **(Pause for 2–3 minutes)**

Having selected five or six experiences of ending from birth to age twelve, choose the most vivid of those experiences. The type of ending is not important; it can be either positive or negative. The only requirement is that it stick out in your memory and command your attention. Open your eyes just long enough to glance at the list and make your selection. **(Pause for 30 seconds)**

In your mind's eye reenter that experience by picturing yourself at that time and at that age. How old were you? . . . Where were you? . . . Who else is there? . . . What is it that is ending and why is that important to you? . . . Let yourself feel what you were feeling then. What are those feelings? . . . Is it sadness you feel? or anger? Or maybe it's a feeling of relief . . . Try to remember how you coped with those feelings. Did anyone talk with you about how you felt? Did you bury your feelings? Was there someone in particular that you turned to for support and encouragement? As you feel ready, express in writing what you feel and think from inside this childhood experience of loss. **(Allow 10–15 minutes for writing)**

Close your eyes again and enter once more the stream of your life. Imagine that you are on a raft that is floating down that portion of the stream of your life from about age twelve to the present. Along the way observe all of the endings that come to your attention. Drift *slowly* through that portion of the stream of your life so that the significant endings along the way can be revealed to you spontaneously. There are all kinds of endings that are likely to appear, both positive and negative— like finishing grade school and high school, or quitting a job that was unrewarding. There will be big endings, like the loss of a loved one through death, a break in an important relationship, or giving up smoking. And there will be little endings, like the end of jury duty or the end of a delightful vacation.

Don't feel rushed as you flow down the stream of your life. Don't avoid the endings which are particularly painful or ignore the endings which are a source of satisfaction to you. We often try to protect ourselves from what is painful, also in our remembering. If you find yourself avoiding a particular ending or experiencing a strong rush of feeling in relation to it, that is a sign that you need to pay attention to this particular ending. On the other hand, we may ignore endings which are gratifying because we assume that loss is always bad and to be deplored. Make a note of those endings which relieved you of a heavy burden. Take a few moments to identify the endings in your life from the time you were twelve to the present. **(Pause for 3–5 minutes)**

From the list which you have assembled choose one of the endings which you have experienced within the recent past. Choose the ending which brings the freshest and strongest feelings, even if that means reaching back to two or three years ago. Recall the circumstances and the people who were involved. What made that ending difficult or perhaps gratifying for you? What were some of your feelings at that time and were you able to turn to someone to help you sort them out? What enabled you to cope with that ending? What was the source of your strength? How did your faith help or hinder your coping with loss? What did you learn from that experience? Do you feel that you grew from it? Is there something that you wish that you had done differently? As you feel ready, express in writing the feelings and thoughts that come out of this recent experience of loss in your life. **(Allow 15–20 minutes for writing)**

## SAYING GOODBYE

*Notes for the Leader*
    What people fear in death is what they fear in life, and the manner in which they cope with losses throughout life will be the way in which they cope with the final losses that come with death. A person who lives with a guilty conscience much of the time will likely be fearful of the final judgment. The person who doesn't like to take a trip unless every detail is worked out in advance will likely fear the unknown when facing death.
    For many people it is the fear of separation that makes death difficult to face. These are people who have a hard time saying goodbye. They unconsciously deny the value which they have attached to the persons, places, and things which they are leaving behind. Instead they focus attention on what lies ahead. They are not comfortable with the feelings of sadness and anger that accompany loss. As a result they rarely complete their goodbyes.
    There is an exercise in Chapter 8 which focuses on the goodbyes which are a part of one's dying. In that exercise participants anticipate some of the separations which would be difficult for them if they were to die, and in the course of the exercise they say goodbye to these people. This exercise on saying goodbye is designed to help participants complete the process of their separation from people, places, and things which have been important to them in the past. Such an experience can not only complete an unfinished process of grieving, but it can also aid the participants in learning how to say goodbye in the future, including the goodbyes that are a part of facing the death of themselves and their loved ones.
    There is no writing portion to this exercise. For this reason, you need to be careful that you do not rush participants through the major transition points within the exercise. I have suggested a method in the exercise for checking on their readiness to continue. Eliminate that if it

seems awkward to you, but be sure that you do not interrupt the process of their imagery before they have brought it to completion.

## Guided Imagery

As you feel ready, let your eyes close so that you can focus your attention on the thoughts and feelings which are genuinely your own . . . letting the peace and quiet of this time and place be a sanctuary for your inward journey . . . letting your breathing come slowly and evenly . . . adjusting the flow of your thoughts and feelings to the natural rhythm of your breathing . . . feeling the unity of mind, body, and spirit . . . letting all of the problems that you have been struggling with fly away . . . feeling only the peace and tranquility of your inner sanctuary.

Resting quietly in the center of yourself, and feeling the safety of being alone with yourself and without fear of intruders, you are ready to revisit people, places, and things which you have left behind but never fully said goodbye to. Let your mind drift back over the years and recall five or six persons who were important to you in the past but are no longer a part of your present life. Choose those persons to whom you never had or took the chance to say goodbye. It may have been a grandparent who died before you were old enough to know just how important he or she was. It may have been a high school chum who helped you make it through adolescence. It may have been a mentor in college or someone you were in love with. As you let your mind drift back over the years, you will be aware of those to whom you have never fully said goodbye, whatever the reason may have been. Make those choices spontaneously without questioning why a particular person comes to your mind. **(Pause for 2–3 minutes)**

Look over the list of persons whom you have placed on your list and choose one to whom you would like to say goodbye. Make your choice according to the strength of your feelings about the importance of this person in your life and the regret that you feel in never saying goodbye. **(Pause for 30 seconds)** Let an image of that person surface in your mind, an image of what that person looked like at the time of your separation from him or her. In your mind's eye, imagine yourself in conversation with this person in a place that you would have likely met when you knew each other. Aware that you will be parting, the purpose of your meeting is to say goodbye. As you look directly at this person who has played an important part in your life, say goodbye in any way that seems appropriate to you. (**Pause for 1–2 minutes**) Listen now to what this person has to say in return and complete the process of saying goodbye. (**Pause for 1–2 minutes**) Keeping your eyes closed, let me know by raising your hand if you need more time to say goodbye. (**Pause for 1 minute if necessary**)

Once again let your mind drift back over the years and recall some of the sacred spaces that have been an important part of your life but are no longer so because of distance or time or both. Choose four or five such places, noting especially those which still generate a strong sense of loss. The church of your childhood might be such a sacred space, or perhaps some other church to which you became strongly attached at some point in your life. The home in which you lived as a child or when you first got married may be a sacred space. Or there may be some special place in nature—in the mountains or by a seashore—that has filled you with a sense of awe and mystery. Choose four or five such places that still evoke strong feelings in you. (**Pause for 1–2 minutes**)

Look over the list of sacred spaces which you have selected and choose one that you would like to revisit for one last time. (**Pause for 30 seconds**) In your mind's eye return to that special place. Capture the feel of that place through what you can see and hear and smell and touch. (**Pause for 30 seconds**) Recall some of the occasions when you were at this place and what it was that made this such an important place. If there are special people associated with this place, let them become part of the experience. If there were special events associated with this place, recall those occasions and the feelings they invoked. (**Pause for 30 seconds**) Now imagine yourself alone in this place, aware that you are there for the last time. Take your leave of this place in any way that seems appropriate to you. It may be something you say or do, or it may be something that is done to you or for you. Let the scene of your farewell unfold spontaneously and naturally without any attempt on your part to have it all make sense and come out a particular way. (**Pause for 1–2 minutes**) Keeping your eyes closed, let me know by raising your hand if you need more time to say goodbye. (**Pause for 1 minute if necessary**)

Let your mind once more drift back over the years, this time to identify possessions which had deep meaning to you. Perhaps it was a bicycle that you had as a child or the first car that you ever owned. Maybe it was something of great sentimental value, a gift from your parents or a good

friend. Choose five or six items which are no longer in your possession but still stir strong memories within you. **(Pause for 1–2 minutes)**
Look over the list which you have assembled and choose one item from among them. In your mind's eye imagine that it is in your possession right now. Picture it as it was when you last owned it. Why was this possession so important to you? What are some of the associations which crowd your mind as you reflect on it? What are some of the circumstances surrounding its loss? Knowing that this is the last time that it will be in your possession, take your leave of this precious possession in any way that seems appropriate to you. **(Pause for 1–2 minutes)**

## LIFE-THREATENING EXPERIENCES

*Notes for the Leader*
The guided imagery exercise on Psalms 90 and 121 in Chapter 6 takes the form of a life-threatening experience while climbing a mountain. It is obviously an imaginary experience since very few people are mountain-climbers. There is an advantage to this kind of imaginary experience. One can surrender fully to the experience because nothing like it has ever happened or is ever likely to happen either to you or someone who is close to you. However, almost everybody has actual life-threatening experiences, some more than others, and some experiences more terrifying than others. Though it may be more difficult to reenter the experience of an actual life-threatening event because of the terror associated with it, there is potential for considerable growth in faith and wisdom by doing so. Life-threatening experiences prompt people to reevaluate their lives and to reorder their priorities. That may be short-lived for those who take little time to reflect on the course of their lives. An exercise like the following is a reminder to remember and offers the possibility of listening once again to what God might be saying through such events.
I used this exercise with a group of college freshmen and discovered that many of them had never had a life-threatening experience that they could remember. This made it difficult for them to relate to the imagery of the exercise. Thus people with more life experience will benefit from this experience more than those who have lived relatively protected lives.
It is important in this exercise that the pace of your speaking be very

deliberate. That is particularly true in that portion of the exercise in which you are asking a series of questions. Long pauses are not needed between questions, but those doing the exercise should never feel rushed.

Many people are eager to share their experience of a life-threatening situation. Some sharing time after this exercise will provide that opportunity for those who could benefit from it. Of course, participants should not be asked to share their experience if they haven't volunteered to do so. Small groups of 3–4 work well for this purpose.

### Guided Imagery

Be aware of your body for a moment. Feel places of tension in your body—perhaps in your shoulders or the back of your neck, perhaps in your lower back or in the pit of your stomach, perhaps a tightness you feel in your head. Wherever it is, let the tension flow away. Stretch your arms and legs, and then let them relax. Rotate your neck around on its axis. Take a deep breath and exhale slowly.

Close your eyes to avoid the distractions of what is going on outside yourself. Let your vision turn inward. As you do so, be aware of your breathing, which continues day and night without conscious intention. It's the natural rhythm of your body, of your inner being. As you attune yourself to this internal rhythm, feel yourself being drawn deeper and deeper into your inner self, feeling the peace and the quiet of this inner sanctuary . . . letting the chair hold the weight of your body . . . letting tension flow from your body like rain water flowing from the roof of a house.

Imagine yourself on the sandy shore of a lake so large that you cannot see to the other side. The beach is deserted except for you and perhaps a friend that you may wish to be there with you. It is in the early morning of a midsummer day. The sun is just beginning to rise over the lake. Some high cumulus clouds over the horizon reflect the brilliant colors of the rising sun. The shimmering waters are like a vast field of sparkling jewels. Allow the peace and beauty of that scene to flood your inner being. Feel the goodness of being alive in such a world. Experience the wonder of God's creation in which water and sky and sun can blend in perfect harmony. **(Pause for 2–3 minutes)**

As you drink in the beauty and wonder of God's creation and

breathe a prayer of thanksgiving that you are privileged to share it, you notice some thunderclouds forming on the horizon. As they come ever nearer, you retreat to the shelter and safety of your beach cabin which is only a hundred yards from shore, there to watch with fascination the developing storm. The dark clouds move quickly over the sky, and the wind begins to blow. With the sudden speed and intensity characteristic of a summer storm, flashing lightning bolts illumine the dark horizon, followed by the crashing sounds of thunder. The roaring wind whips the sea into a fury, and huge waves roll over the beach. The blissful summer morning has turned into an awesome and frightening display of nature's power and potential destructiveness.

As you watch the storm within the safe shelter of the cabin, your thoughts turn to the beauty and fragility of life in God's order of creation. You know that your life would be in danger if you were on the lake in a small craft during that raging storm, and your thoughts turn naturally to times when your life was threatened. Letting your mind drift back over the years, recall occasions when your life felt threatened. It may be that the threat was not as great as you thought it was at that time. What's important is that you felt it to be life-threatening. It need not have been a sudden and dramatic threat to your life, like a car accident or being in a small boat on a storm-tossed lake. It may have been a threat which grew with the passing of time, like a fear of serious physical ailment or fear of losing your mind. List four to six such experiences if there have been that many. Just a word or a phrase is all that you will need to identify the experience you have in mind and then close your eyes. Let your choices be spontaneous. Trust your intuitions about which experiences were really life-threatening. **(Pause for 2–3 minutes)**

When you have completed your list of life-threatening experiences, look over the list and choose the one which still evokes the most terror when you think about it. **(Pause for 30 seconds)** When you have made your choice, go back to the time when you first became aware of the threat to your life. You will be able to reenter that experience with the aid of your memory and imagination. Recall some of the circumstances which led up to the awareness that your life was in danger. Was it sudden or something that only slowly dawned on you, or perhaps something you were aware of only after the threat was past? Was it a threat to you alone or were there other people involved? Let yourself fully enter that experience once again. What are your feelings? Are you frightened? How do you cope with the situation? Do you turn to others for help or face it all by yourself? Where is God in this experience? Are you aware of his presence? Do you turn to him for help? **(Pause for 2–3 minutes)**

As you reflect on the meaning of that experience for your life now, what difference does it make? Has it made you more aware of the value of your life in the present? Does it make any difference in the priorities that you have? How would you change your life if you had only one more year to live? one more month? one more week? What relationships seem most important to you when you think about having only a short time to live? What would you want to happen in those relationships? What, if anything, would you change in your relationship to God if you had one year to live? one month? one week? Would you change your worship habits? your prayer life? your behavior? If your answer is yes, why would you make those changes? Because of fear? Because of a different understanding of yourself? Because of a reordering of priorities?

As you are ready, express in writing the feelings and thoughts which emerge from the inner recesses of your being. Write from within the life-threatening experience, describing what it means for your life and faith to be aware that your life could end at any time. Let the feelings and thoughts flow spontaneously from what is inside of you. **(Allow 15– 20 minutes for writing)**

## UNSTRUCTURED MEDITATION

### Notes for the Leader

Most of the exercises in this book are fairly structured. Specific images are provided, though there is also the opportunity for each individual to supply imagery from his or her own experience. The following exercise is unstructured in that each individual is given maximum flexibility to chart whatever area of experience in relation to death and dying that seems appropriate at the time.

### Guided Imagery

Sitting in quiet and calm . . . letting your body become heavy and your spirit light. As your eyes gently close, let your breathing come evenly and slowly. As the stillness deepens, let your mind slow its pace, adjusting its rhythm to the tempo of your breathing. Breathing moves in and out, quieting the body and the mind with its steady rhythm . . . bringing stillness and peace to the inner self . . . letting the concerns and problems of the day float away like balloons carried aloft by gentle winds . . . hearing the sounds of silence . . . feeling the soft beauty of the interior world which beckons you deeper and deeper into the center of your self.

Resting quietly in the center of yourself . . . calmly waiting in openness for what is to come . . . knowing that you can see more deeply into things than before . . . that you can hear more than your ear could ever discern, that you can know the truth at the core of your being as you never did before . . . resting quietly in the center of yourself, you are aware of the presence of the Spirit of God within you . . . waiting calmly in the center of yourself . . . feeling the rhythm of your steady, even breathing.

As the stillness and calm deepen within you, you find yourself in a forest with trees so tall that they seem to reach to the sky. The branches of the trees, high above you, provide a covering that looks like the vaulted ceiling of a cathedral. The bright sun cannot reach the cool forest floor where you walk with bare feet on lush green grass fed by an underground spring. There is quiet and a peaceful calm all around you as you walk in the lush grass of the forest floor.

Feeling the mystery of this forest cathedral, you know that you are no longer alone. A shaft of sunlight bursts through an opening in the cathedral ceiling of overlapping branches. The beam of sunlight falls directly on a huge gleaming white stone that stands in an opening of the forest, spreading light on every side of it.

You are standing deep in the forest. It is dark at the floor of the forest, except for the soft light that is reflected from the huge white stone that stands at the center of the forest. The soft quality of the light is calming and quieting and assuring. In the light you feel a power and a presence that is both in and beyond the light, a presence that does not diminish, a light that glows wherever there is darkness.

As you stand before the mighty stone at the center of the forest, able to see its soft light only with the eyes of your inner self, you hear a voice in the stillness of the forest which you can only hear with the ears of your inner self. Filled with a sense of awe and mystery at being in this holy place, you listen carefully to the voice which speaks out of the silence only to you, letting the mystery of the beyond in our midst become more and more real to you. As the experience deepens and as you feel ready, express in writing what comes to you from within the experience about the meaning of life, and about death, and about what lies beyond death. Let the writing be free and uninhibited by interpretation or critical analysis. Let the writing flow from what you experience of the presence of God deep within you. **(Allow 20–25 minutes for writing)**

## DUAL IMAGERY

*Notes for the Leader*

Dual imagery can be used to increase awareness of images within oneself which are in dialectical tension with each other. Though they are opposites, the images may be complementary, each highlighting a different aspect of the interior world. Several suggestions for dual imagery exercises will be made in this section. Some form of induction is needed for each, either one of your own making or an adaptation of one from another of the exercises in this book.

### Death as Enemy and Death as Friend

*Guided Imagery*

Let an image of death as your enemy form in your mind. It may be an image of death which you recall from some artist's conception of death in the form of a skeleton, gaping jaws, or a monster. It may be an image which you create out of your own unconscious fear of death. As that image forms in your mind, be aware of the feelings within yourself that are triggered by that image. What is it that frightens you about the image? Why is it your enemy?

Let that image of death recede in your consciousness and let another image form of death as your friend. This may be an image which is harder for you to form because most of the time death is imaged as an enemy and a stranger. Try to imagine a situation where death would be welcomed and then wait for an image to form. It may be an image like those described by people who have had near-death experiences: floating free, going through a tunnel, welcomed by a friend. It may be an image which you create out of your own unconscious anticipation of the goodness of death. As that image forms in your mind, be aware of the feelings within yourself that are triggered by that image. What is it that is comforting about the image? Why is it your friend?

Now let these two images come together in the same chamber of your mind. If both of the images are personal in form, have them speak to each other and record the dialogue which unfolds. If the images are very different in form, respond first to one and then to the other so that the two different ways you feel and think about death may be held in close juxtaposition. Images of death as enemy and death as friend are both products of your imagination. Listen carefully to what each has to say to you.

## A Battle for Your Soul

### *Notes for the Leader*

In the late medieval period there were frequent artistic representations of a battle between angels and demons over the souls of Christians who were dying. It was believed that the fate of the soul was determined at the time of death. It could be expected that the temptations of Satan would be particularly strong at the time of death, but one could also count on the promise of God to send his angels to guard the soul in its journey to the bosom of Abraham. Though Satanic imagery is not as common to Christians today, the dialectical tension between what Luther called ''the old self'' and ''the new self'' in Christians is still very strong.

### *Guided Imagery*

Imagine at the time of your death a confrontation between an angel, however you wish to image this emissary from the kingdom of light and eternal life, and a demon, however you wish to image this emissary from the kingdom of darkness and eternal death. Imagine the confrontation not in the form of a battle, each fighting for the possession of your soul, as it is often depicted in medieval art, but as a reasoned argument about the fate of your soul. With the aid of your imagination, let that argument unfold spontaneously and record it in writing. Avoid pre-judgments and doctrinal formulations. Let the argument over the fate of your soul flow out of the interior consciousness of your inner self with your pen simply recording the flow of that consciousness.

## Facing the Death of Yourself

### Guided Imagery I

Imagine that you are in a boat in the middle of the ocean. You look over the side of the boat and see someone struggling in the water. As you look more closely at the person, you recognize the person in the water as you. What do you do? Let the drama unfold in your imagination. **(Pause for 1–2 minutes)** After the drama is completed, imagine that the "you" who was on the boat and the "you" who was in the water are seated in easy chairs facing each other in conversation about what happened. Let that conversation unfold spontaneously and record its outcome in writing.

### Guided Imagery II

Imagine that you are terminally ill and close to the time of your death. You have been surrounded by family and friends, all of whom have provided support and loving care. You have had an opportunity to say goodbye to each of them. They have all left the room. Through the door comes another person and approaches your bed. You recognize the person to be yourself. What does he or she have to say to you? What do you have to say in return? Let the dialogue flow freely and spontaneously without making any judgments about what is said. Record the conversation in writing between the you who is dying and the you who is responding to the person who is dying.